D1045091

THE UPSIDE OF FEAR

How One Man Broke the Cycle of Prison, Poverty, and Addiction

WELDON LONG

GREENLEAF BOOK GROUP PRESS

Published by Greenleaf Book Group Press
Austin, TX
www.greenleafbookgroup.com

Distributed by Greenleaf Book Group LLC

For ordering information or special discounts for bulk purchases, please contact Greenleaf Book Group LLC at PO Box 91869, Austin, TX 78709, (512)891-6100

Design and composition by Greenleaf Book Group LLC
Cover design by Greenleaf Book Group LLC

Publisher's Cataloging-In-Publication Data
(Prepared by The Donohue Group, Inc.)

Long, Weldon.
The upside of fear : how one man broke the cycle of prison, poverty, and addiction / Weldon Long. -- 1st ed.

p. ; cm.

ISBN: 978-1-60832-000-4

1. Long, Weldon. 2. Criminals--Colorado--Biography. 3. Addicts--Colorado--Effect of imprisonment on. 4. Businessmen--Colorado--Biography. 5. Life change events. I. Title.

HV6248.L66 A3 2009
364.1/092 2009925204

Part of the Tree Neutral™ program, which offsets the number of trees consumed in the production and printing of this book by taking proactive steps, such as planting trees in direct proportion to the number of trees used: www.treeneutral.com

Printed in the United States of America on acid-free paper

16 17 18 19 20 21 10 9 8 7 6 5 4 3

First Edition

Contents

Acknowledgments v

Preface ix

1 A Night Out with Elliot: Spring 1987 1

2 Black Monday: October 19, 1987 13

3 Me: 1964 to 1987 23

4 I'm Going to Cañon City, Cañon City Here I Come . . . :
December 1987 to Spring 1990 29

5 Back on the Street Again:
Spring 1990 to December 1, 1991 41

6 And Then There Were Two:
December 1, 1991 to January 1993 57

7 Happy Birthday to Me: January 18, 1993 67

8 Back to the Can:
January 1993 to Fall 1993 75

9 Back on the Street Again (Reprise):
Fall 1993 to March 1995 83

10 Viva Las Vegas:
March 1995 to March 1996 91

11 The Turning Point:
March 1996 to August 1996. 101

12 The Upside of Fear:
September 1996 to August 1997. 113

13 Reality Bites:
December 1996 to July 1997 127

14 Not Out of the Woods Yet:
August 1997 to May 1999 135

15 Finished with the Feds:
May 14, 1999 to December 10, 1999 151

16 The Prodigal Son Returns to Cañon City:
December 10, 1999 to October 2002 159

17 Back on the Streets Again (Final Reprise):
October 2002 to April 2003 179

18 Epilogue:
2003 to Present. 189

Acknowledgments

EVERYONE IS AFRAID OF SOMETHING.

I was afraid of everything.

Sitting here on the lanai of our Maui home, looking out over the manicured fairways of the Bay Course at Kapalua and the deep blue water of the Pacific Ocean, I have finally found the peace of mind to do something that people have been encouraging me to do for years—write my life story. But I would not have been able to produce this book, or even survive my own self-destruction, if it had not been for the support of many people.

I'd first like to thank my mother, Mary Wainwright Goudeau, who supported and loved me even when I was undeserving. I love you, Mom. To my father, Richard Long, Sr.—I love you more than you knew and would give up everything to have one more day with you. To my siblings Susan, Richard (and Eloise), and David—I love you and thank you for the love and friendship you have given me. To my sister Annette—we all love and miss you. My love and thanks to Grandmother Long as well. Thanks to the New Orleans Saints for giving me something to cheer and hope for and for always connecting me to home—WHO DAT! My thanks and love to Nana and Papa Jack Ilgen, who always accepted my collect calls, and to the rest of the Hamlin/Whitson family for taking care of Hunter while I went insane. To Chris, Josh, and Andrew: I wish I had been a better man when you were young, and I am proud of the men you've become.

My thanks to everyone at ITSUP2U Media for doing such a great job and making our business awesome.

Special thanks to my best friend on this planet, Charlie Beckham. You were there with me in my darkest moments, and I'll always treasure your friendship. Baby Christopher is lucky to have you as his dad.

Thanks to everyone at Greenleaf, especially Bill Crawford, who made this project unbelievably easy once I convinced him to stop "red lining" my work. Thanks to Justin Branch and John Rogan for dinner and getting excited about this project. My sincere thanks to Theresa Reding for making my story infinitely easier to read and to Sheila Parr for the beautiful and intriguing design work—makes me want to read this damn thing one more time.

I would like to thank Jo Ann Cole, Vince and Pattie Stephens, Martha, Gil, Chandler, Bailey Blood, and Hunter Cole. Very, very special thanks to Jo Ann for introducing me to the paradise of Napili Kai.

Thanks to Mick Fleetwood and the Island Rumors Band and Kalapana for inspiring me under the Maui stars one summer night to get this book done. You never know when your music will touch a stranger, do you?

Thanks to Patrick Shaw for teaching me that there is no time for whining and excuses and that affirmations work to ensure success in any endeavor . . . even golf. And speaking of golf, thanks to all the guys in the "Bill Cardone Golf Club" for bringing me along for the ride. For a guy like me who never had many friends, the Golf

Trips are special times . . . even when Frank accidentally kills innocent animals. Finally, thanks to Diane Ward and Christine Kaberna for reviewing the earliest manuscript, and thanks to Darren Kaberna for letting us keep the house key.

Thanks to Dr. Wayne Dyer, Napoleon Hill, Stephen Covey, Anthony Robbins, and Viktor Frankl. Your words saved my life.

Also a word of gratitude must go to Tom Ramunda, the best criminal defense attorney in Colorado. If not for your aggressive, brilliant legal work, my dreams could never have become a reality. Thanks for saving my ass.

Thanks to Chief Judge Gilbert Martinez for giving me one more chance.

To Janet, I will always love you for taking a chance and believing in a long shot like me.

And to my son, Hunter, this story would never have happened without you. You gave me the motivation and strength to press on in my darkest hours. Because of you, I never gave up. I am so proud of the young man you have become, and I love you more than any father has ever loved a son.

And the greatest thanks of all goes to God for saving me from certain self-destruction and showing me the path out of darkness.

And finally, my sincere heartfelt apologies go to all those who were victims of my crimes and my insanity. I had no right to do the things I did. I am truly sorry.

Preface

MAUI IS NICER THAN PRISON.

I know this because I was in prison for thirteen years, and today I own a home on Maui.

Prisons are a lot of things, all of them bad. They are ugly. They breed violence, sometimes horrific violence. They foster scams of all types. Prisons serve bad food, of course, but mostly they offer nothing—just daily, mind-numbing emptiness and loneliness. No matter how it is depicted in the movies, prison is a very boring place. There just isn't much good to say about prison. You can see why I prefer Maui.

Prison is also about thousands of men packed together, living lives of quiet, and sometimes not so quiet, desperation. Prisoners are desperate men—desperate for different things, to be sure, but each one is desperate for something. I was no different.

I was desperate for peace and prosperity. Not peace and prosperity for the whole world, mind you, just peace and prosperity for me. Mostly, I just wanted prosperity. In time I learned that to have peace and prosperity for myself I had to want it for others as well, but that's getting way ahead of my story.

My story is not really about prison or Maui. It's about the ideas and concepts that transformed my life while I was incarcerated. It's about how anyone can use a few simple tools to create spiritual, emotional, and financial health. It's about having no limits. It's about embracing a concept I call The Upside of Fear and using it to create the life of your dreams, no matter how you may be living today.

When I left prison in 2003 I was a thirty-nine-year-old "three-time loser." I had spent thirteen years, practically my entire adult life, in prisons, jails, and halfway houses. I had stolen hundreds of thousands of dollars, yet I was broke. For twenty years I lived a selfish and destructive life, oblivious to the pain I caused others and myself. I drank, drugged, robbed, lied, and spent every dime that I could grab. That's what I did.

Society was perfectly justified in not expecting anything different from me after I was released in 2003.

How could they know something had changed deep inside me? How could anyone know how the final seven years of incarceration had changed my life?

But by the time I was released from my third prison tour in 2003, things *had* changed. *I* had changed. Instead of doing what I had always done—drinking, drugging, and committing crimes—I got clean and sober. I committed myself to achieving success and building a life based on hard work, integrity, and personal responsibility. And although the change I made within myself may seem trivial, the visible results of that change were stunning.

That change is what this book is about.

While in prison from 1996 to 2003, I began to want something more out of life. So I tried an experiment. I began to read. I read every kind of success and personal development book I could get my hands on—Christian, Buddhist, atheist or Mormon, I didn't care.

I decided to try the things I read about and see what happened. Maybe my life would improve. I had absolutely nothing to lose.

Nothing could have prepared me for the success of this experiment.

I began to *write* down what I wanted my life to look like. I began to *visualize* and embrace what was at first only a fantasy. Despite being a high school dropout, I visualized having an education. Despite being homeless, I visualized having beautiful homes in the mountains of Colorado and on the beaches of Maui. Despite being penniless, I visualized having wealth. Despite being a thief and a liar, I visualized being a man of character and integrity. Despite being alone, I visualized the love of a beautiful, honorable woman. Despite being fifty pounds overweight and lethargic, I visualized being thin and active. Despite the fact that two different men and my drug-addicted wife were raising my son, I visualized my son living a healthy, stable life with me.

I began to *act* in a manner consistent with what I claimed I wanted. I accepted who I was and stopped pretending I was someone I wasn't. I began to tell the truth. I became willing to believe there was a benevolent God that wanted good things for me. I came to know that if I used the Law of Attraction, the outcome would take care of itself.

Above all, I took *responsibility* for the quality and circumstances of my life. No longer would I be a victim of circumstances. No longer would I be at the mercy of the system. I accepted the fact that I alone had created the quality of my life, and I alone had the capability to change it. So I did.

In a few short years after being released from prison, all of my visualizations manifested themselves in my life as if by magic. The people and events that had first appeared in my mind's eye became a reality. My circumstances and my spirit changed so dramatically that those who knew me when I was a total loser could not believe how my new life was unfolding.

I had a hard time believing it myself.

Before leaving prison I received my BS in law and an MBA in management (yes, I went to Jail not Yale). Within four years of my release from prison, I owned the largest and fastest growing residential heating and air conditioning company in Colorado. I was living in my dream home on a golf course in the mountains west of Colorado Springs, raising my son, Hunter, in a healthy, stable home. And now, as I begin to write this story, I am sitting in the tropical paradise of Maui, sipping a cup of freshly brewed Hawaiian coffee. Pretty amazing, isn't it?

How was any of this—much less *all* of this—possible? How did a career criminal, a high school dropout who never achieved anything, go from poverty, addiction, hopelessness, crime, and prison to a productive and honorable life within a few short years?

I changed my thoughts. And when I changed my thoughts, I changed the way I felt. And when I changed the way I felt, I changed the way I acted. And when I changed the way I acted, I got better results.

Now, instead of living a desperate life in my prison cell, separated from civilization by concrete walls and razor wire, I live a life of success and integrity. Instead of "walking the yard" in a high-security prison, I'm walking the beaches of Maui, barefoot, with the Pacific Ocean lapping over my feet. Instead of wasting my life and hurting innocent people, I'm writing a book about how I used ideas to transform my miserable existence into a life that matters.

I like this new life of mine.

The events in this story are true. Some of it is deadly serious, some of it is funny, and some of it is terribly sad. But every word is true.

I hope that my story will encourage you to reach for the dreams of your youth. I hope you will come to understand that if I could dramatically change my life, you can too. Within these pages is a plan that will enable you to transform your own life. The only things necessary on your part are desire and commitment. If you are willing to open your mind to The Upside of Fear, your life can be awesome. If you are broke, you can become wealthy. If you are lonely, you can find companionship. If you are overweight, you can become fit and healthy. If you are tired, you can find rest. If you are anxious, you can find peace.

I know you can, because I did. And I am just an average guy living a spectacular life.

CHAPTER 1
A Night Out with Elliot

Spring 1987

THE MOMENT I SLID OUT OF MY TRUCK with the gun in my hand, I knew I was in way over my head. Not just a little over my head. So far over my head that my life would never be the same.

My life was already pretty much shit, but it was about to get considerably worse.

In May 1987, I was a lazy twenty-three-year-old slug who spent my waking hours drinking. Boozing it up. I was particularly fond of Jack Daniel's Old Time Tennessee Whiskey, which on most days I would start sipping around midmorning. My work never interfered with my drinking, as I had none—work that is.

I had lost a business the year before due to my excessive drinking and some really bad financial management, and I wasn't quite ready to jump back into the workforce. My wife, on the other hand, was a hard worker, and she waitressed to support us. This freed me to wallow in self-pity and misery and sip my Jack Daniel's. Although I had never worked as a mind reader, something told me she just barely managed to tolerate me.

Since I didn't have a job, whatever rent money I managed to scrounge up each month I'd blow on liquor and playing darts at a local pub. There always seemed to be just enough money for booze. Ah, the good life.

But this night, the rent was overdue, and I didn't quite have the money together. So I'd been out hitting the pawnshops on East Colfax in Denver, Colorado, trying to pawn the shotgun my wife had given me on our first anniversary a year and a half earlier. I guess I'm a little sentimental that way.

After a few pawnbrokers offered me only about 10 percent of the gun's value in cash, I decided to go with plan B. Plan B was simple: I'd get drunk and drive around the sleazy parts of Denver until I figured out what to do.

While driving around I stopped to buy some cocaine from a guy on a street corner. I thought I'd get a better idea of what to do about the rent money if I complemented my drinking with smoking a little crack. I had never smoked crack before, but this would be one of many firsts this night. I had an ice chest full of beer in the truck, which would have been plenty of fuel for most folks trying to come up with landlord money, but I wanted more. Smoking cocaine with a stranger in a dangerous part of town somehow seemed like more.

I was still working on plan B when I picked up a slender, black hitchhiker named Elliot. To this day I have no idea what made me stop and give him a ride. I never picked up hitchhikers.

Elliot and I partied, drinking and smoking more crack, while I drove him where he needed to go. When we arrived at a simple house just east of inner-city Denver, Elliot said he didn't really have any pressing business and asked if he could hang out for a while. I was always ready to keep the party going, and Elliot seemed like a nice guy, so instead of me dropping him off, we drove away.

The next several hours are pretty vague. I remember a lot of drinking and smoking cocaine as we continued to cruise aimlessly around east Denver. But then we began to talk about money. We were out of cash and needed to get more alcohol and drugs. I mentioned the anniversary shotgun I had stashed behind the seat, and we started talking about how we could use it to solve our money problem. Since pawning it hadn't worked out, our conversation casually turned to using it for armed robbery. We might as well have been talking about getting a burger at the drive through—it was that matter-of-fact. We were running low on alcohol and drugs and gas, and taking money from someone else—at gunpoint—seemed like a perfectly legitimate way to keep the party going.

When I was a teenager, I had stolen petty cash from the truck stop where I worked after school, but I wasn't exactly a hardened criminal. My larceny was never discovered, but perhaps if it had been, I would have learned a lesson as a teenager that would have prevented significant pain for me as an adult. I remember hoping I would never get caught lifting twenty dollars from the till, not knowing that I should be careful what I wished for.

Now, plotting armed robbery with Elliot just seemed to be the sensible thing to do. It didn't occur to me that the booze and cocaine might be affecting my judgment. With a little luck we might even steal enough to pay my overdue rent. I had figured out my plan B.

"Hey," I told Elliot. "We could be a modern-day Butch Cassidy and the Sundance Kid." Elliot liked that idea. We joked about how cool it was when the Hole in the Wall Gang stole money, but we couldn't agree on who would be Butch and who would be Sundance. Eventually the conversation got serious. A blue and red Domino's Pizza sign caught my eye, and I suggested we make that our target.

"No," Elliot said. "Someone from the neighborhood might recognize me. Why don't we go to another part of the city?"

"Hey, we should go north to Wyoming," I suggested. "Didn't Butch and Sundance go through Wyoming?"

"No way," Elliot said. "The second those damn cowboys see a black man walk in, they'll know somethin's up." I thought Elliot was full of shit, but then again, I'd never been a black man in cowboy country. So much for Wyoming.

We decided to head south down Interstate 25 to Colorado Springs. As we drove through the night, with Van Halen's "Jump" playing in the background, Elliot and I got quiet. I don't think we were sobering up: I think we were both beginning to realize that we were going to go through with it. We didn't know exactly what "it" was, but we knew something serious was going to happen. And somewhere in the back of our drug-addled minds, we were having second thoughts.

I sensed that Elliot was beginning to get a little nervous. I surmised he didn't like Van Halen as much as I did, which should have told me right away there was something wrong with him. We decided to make a move and exited the interstate about thirty miles south of Denver.

We pulled into a liquor store parking lot and tried to work up our nerve. Through the window, I watched the clerk going about his business, oblivious to what was about to happen.

Then something occurred to me. "Hey," I asked Elliot, "don't liquor store guys have guns?"

"Maybe."

Now I was nervous, too. We weren't looking for a fair fight. We wanted better odds. So we backed away slowly from the liquor store and jumped back on the interstate, continuing south toward Colorado Springs.

As we headed down the highway, my second thoughts about plan B grew. But it was nothing significant enough to stop me from what I was about to do. I wasn't afraid of committing a robbery or of getting arrested. I just had a nagging feeling that I was officially about to become a seriously worthless piece of shit.

Despite these doubts, I continued to drive. It was about 10:00 PM. We pulled into Colorado Springs and spotted an upscale restaurant. We parked in front of the eatery and refined our strategy. We decided to rob the next group of people who walked out of the place. Some refinement. Elliot grabbed the shotgun. I picked up an old pellet gun I kept under the seat of my truck for harassing neighborhood cats or shattering windows for kicks. We were armed and ready. I knew this time we wouldn't back out.

As we waited in the darkness of the parking lot, my misgivings continued to nag at me. I realized that if I stepped out of the truck there would be no turning back. My parents were good, hardworking middle-class people who had tried to raise me right. I knew better than to think that stealing was an acceptable solution to my financial problems. I knew once I committed myself to this crime, I was crossing a distinct boundary between good and evil. I knew that after crossing that line, regret and remorse might help assuage my guilt, but I would eventually have to answer to the universal laws of consequence and accountability. What was I going to do?

Two men exited the restaurant. I eased the door open. Elliot and I slid out of the truck. We charged across the parking lot toward the two men, yelling like Indians on the warpath.

Committing any crime is stupid, but this one was especially moronic. Elliot and I never stopped to consider whether anyone other than our victims would hear or see us or notice my bright red pickup. Would our two victims actually be carrying anything valuable? We really had no idea what we were doing.

"Stop right fucking there!" Elliot screamed. The two men froze as we leveled our guns at them. "Give us your money, motherfuckers!"

"Don't be a fucking hero!" I heard another voice shout. "Just give him the goddamn money!" *Who was that idiot who was yelling?*

It was me. That was *my* voice. But how could that be? I had always considered myself a nice guy. I had never hurt anyone before. I had never even been in a fight, except for that time in the fourth grade when a classmate pushed me over a trash can. Yet there I stood, threatening to kill two guys who were minding their own business, enjoying a meal.

"Take it easy, take it easy," said one of the victims, a nicely dressed, middle-aged man. "There's no reason to get excited. What do you want? Our wallets? Our watches?"

Our victims didn't resist for a moment. They handed over their jewelry and billfolds as quickly as they could, trying to calm us down. I don't blame them. I can only imagine the panic these two guys were feeling as two gun-waving petty thieves threatened to shoot them down in a dark, cold parking lot. These guys had a lot more to live for than their money and credit cards.

As Elliot grabbed the men's valuables, reality hit me. I wanted away from the parking lot. I wanted away from Elliot. I wanted to cross back over the line between evil and good. I wanted out. I wasn't anywhere near accepting that it was too late for that.

I bolted for the truck. I thought that if I could put enough distance between myself and the scene, the whole incident would disappear. One part of me believed that it wasn't even really happening. But it was happening, and I had to escape.

I jumped in the truck, started the engine, and threw it into gear. Just as I started to pull out of the parking lot, Elliot dove in. *How the hell did he catch me?* I thought.

"Come on, man," I shouted. "Get your ass in here!" I didn't want him to think I was double-crossing him. He was, after all, carrying a loaded shotgun. Lucky for me, Elliot didn't seem to notice that I had tried to split. Maybe he'd turned to run just when I did. Or maybe he bolted in order to steal my truck and leave me in the parking lot to explain things to the police. Elliot and I had some pretty serious trust issues.

We sped away from the parking lot. *The interstate—just get to the goddamn interstate*, I thought to myself. *The interstate equals getting away. Get to the interstate.*

We were almost there. I started breathing a little easier. I began negotiating a deal with God to let me get out of this mess when suddenly, there they were. Headlights. Bright, right-on-my-ass headlights blasting the rearview mirror. It looked like a van. A goddamn van was following me and flashing its headlights. "Who the fuck is that?" I asked, as if Elliot would know.

Suddenly it hit me.

Someone had witnessed the crime, and they were chasing us. They weren't going to let us get away. My negotiations with God had apparently hit a snag. Who were these guys? If they had seen what we had done, then surely they must know we had guns. Were they crazy?

As we entered the on-ramp to the interstate, I gave up trying to escape. I made up my mind to surrender, but only to the cops, not to the people chasing us. I didn't know who was in that van, but I wasn't going to turn myself over to a gang of vigilantes. I appreciated the irony of the situation. The hunters were now the hunted. I was now hoping that the cops would show up to protect me from the van people.

I decided to stay on the interstate, heading straight north, and drive at about 45 miles per hour. That would keep me safe from the vigilantes and provide a steady, predictable course for the police to target. I also remembered that there was a Colorado State Police office about thirty miles up the interstate in Castle Rock. As a last resort I could pull into the State Police office and surrender. I would be safe there.

I was a serious badass, hoping the cops would protect me from the do-gooders in the van. How pathetic.

Elliot had a different plan. As I poked along I-25, he looked up from counting the less than twenty dollars we had collected in the robbery and shouted, "Speed up, you stupid son of a bitch. What the fuck is your problem?"

"I'm not going anywhere is what the fuck my problem is, asshole," I responded. "Twenty bucks isn't worth dying over. Those assholes behind us might have guns, too, and as long as we're not making an effort to get away, maybe they'll wait for the cops to arrest us and not shoot us in the back of our fucking heads." It sounded sensible enough to me, but I wasn't getting through to Elliot.

"Motherfucker!" Elliot screamed. "*I'll* shoot your dumb ass if you don't get me the fuck out of here right now!" He stuck the loaded shotgun into my ribs.

I grabbed the barrel with my right hand as I held the steering wheel with my left. "If you shoot me, we'll crash. And those crazy van people will either hold us for the cops or shoot our dumb asses."

Elliot put the gun down, but he wasn't convinced that I was right. He stomped my foot down on the accelerator.

"Come on, you stupid motherfucker. Let's go!" he screamed.

"Look!" I yelled back at him, fighting to regain control. "I am not going to get myself killed. Not by the cops, not by the crazy motherfuckers behind us, and not by you!" Elliot removed his foot from the accelerator. "Here's what I'll do. I'll pull over on the shoulder where it's really dark, and you can get out of the truck and hide in the ditch. Hopefully the van people will stay far enough behind so they can't see you. Then I'll take off, the van will follow me, and you'll be a free man. No one will ever know who you are. *I* don't even know who the fuck you are!"

Elliot mulled the idea over as we drove slowly up I-25. Finally he said, "All right, I'll do it."

Thank God, I thought, *one less asshole to worry about.*

Elliot removed the interior dome light so it wouldn't turn on when he opened the door. I eased over to the shoulder, gradually slowing to a stop. The van stopped a long way behind us—at least a hundred yards or so. It was very dark. Elliot began to get out of the truck. My plan was working beautifully.

Then Elliot froze. "I'm not getting stuck out here," he mumbled. "No fucking way." Suddenly, he grabbed the shotgun, jumped out of the truck, aimed toward the van, and fired.

"Holy shit!" I screamed. "Have you lost your fucking mind?"

Elliot jumped back in. We careened back onto the interstate. Elliot didn't have to tell me to go fast. My heart pounded and my ears rang. The shotgun blast reverberated in my head. It was over. Everything was over. We were murderers.

Then the van reappeared behind us. Could Elliot have missed his target? *Please*, I prayed, *let Elliot be a lousy shot*. It was time to try a second round of negotiations with the Almighty. *God, don't let anyone die*.

The van followed patiently but kept a little more distance between us.

I slowed down. The van people followed us through the dark. At least twenty minutes had passed since we'd left the restaurant, but still no cops. They couldn't be far off, could they? We were halfway to Castle Rock.

Elliot sat still. We drove slowly through the night, waiting for the police. Suddenly Elliot seemed to accept our fate, and we quietly awaited the consequences. Everything was silent.

As we approached the State Police office in Castle Rock, the police finally appeared. Patrol cars were everywhere—on the overpass, on the shoulders, and on the exit ramps. Flashing blue and red lights lit up the sky like a carnival. The cops were ready for Butch and Sundance.

I pulled onto the shoulder and stopped the truck. Patrol cars surrounded me, blocking traffic on the interstate. I slowly opened my door, stepped out, put my hands high in the air, and awaited instructions.

"Lay facedown on the pavement," a voice boomed through the night. "Keep your hands above your head."

I followed instructions as if my life depended on it—clearly it did. As I lay facedown in the center of the road, I could almost feel the guns trained on me. No sudden moves. I felt open, exposed, and humiliated, lying facedown in the middle of Interstate 25, a pathetic, incompetent criminal, getting his just desserts.

"Get out of the vehicle, or we'll shoot."

Come on Elliot, I thought to myself, *get out of the fucking truck*. I wasn't really worried about Elliot. I was worried that I was lying down a few feet away from a guy who was about to become Swiss cheese. In that moment, I became a strong supporter of extensive law enforcement training. Rule number one: Don't shoot the guy who followed instructions. Rule number two: Only shoot the other guy. Rule number three: Be a really, really good shot.

Elliot finally stepped out onto the highway. The police swarmed us and took us into custody "without incident." Apparently, Elliot's procrastination did not qualify as an incident.

Surrounded by police on the side of the interstate, I lost track of Elliot. Before long I was handcuffed, placed in the back of a police cruiser, and driven back to Colorado Springs.

I stared silently out the window as we headed south.

Later that night, I sat in a holding cell with my head in my hands as a detective brought the victims in to identify me. I tried to hide my face, but I finally followed the detective's instructions and raised my head. I was sick with shame and embarrassment.

I was booked into the El Paso County jail and charged with aggravated armed robbery, attempted murder, and a crime of violence. Things had gotten pretty serious. I had nearly killed two men, and

I was facing up to forty-eight years in prison. I still didn't have the rent money.

I spent the next few days desperately trying to get out of jail. When my bond was set at $50,000, I did the only thing I could think of. I called my mother and begged for help like a small child. I had been able to manipulate my mother my entire life, yet this time she was reluctant to lend me a hand. I had gotten in way over my head. Family members and my mother's lawyer advised her not to get involved. They told her to let me suffer the consequences of my actions.

As the days passed, I grew more desperate. To make my mother believe I was in danger, I lied and told her that someone was taking my food and threatening my life. Although others could see right through my deception, my mother finally gave in and arranged for my bail. As I waited for the legal action to proceed, I wondered if I would be able to con the judge as easily as I had always been able to con my mother.

A month later I wore a good-looking suit to the courtroom for my preliminary hearing. I guess I cleaned up pretty well, because the victims, the van people, and the cops who arrested me mistook me for one of the lawyers at the defense table. Although the victims had identified me the night of my arrest, without a formal identification in court at the preliminary hearing, the state couldn't prosecute me, so they had cut a deal with Elliot.

Elliot was shackled in handcuffs, wearing a county lockup orange jumpsuit. Apparently he had not made bail and was still in custody. He looked different than he had on our night out together—less menacing and less threatening. In fact, he looked rather slight in his oversize jumpsuit.

As Elliot and I stood together in court, he identified me as his cohort. In exchange for Elliot's testimony, the state dismissed the attempted murder charges filed against him. It was the first and last time I saw Elliot after the robbery. I don't hold any grudges against him. If he hadn't identified me, the state would have figured out some other way to move the prosecution forward. It just seemed like an odd way to say, "Thanks for the ride, buddy."

According to my lawyer, the two men we robbed that night were local businessmen out for a quiet dinner. Even after what I had done to them, they weren't out for vengeance. In fact, they even wanted to offer me a job if I wasn't sent to prison. Their level of compassion after what I'd done to them amazed me.

The local media and law enforcement recognized the van people as heroes. I'd say they deserved at least that. After witnessing the robbery, they were determined not to let us get away. Elliot's shotgun blast shattered their windshield but didn't penetrate the glass, and the shot only made them more determined to follow us.

I'm grateful, of course, that no one was killed that spring night in 1987. If that had happened, I would have faced charges of first-degree murder—probably even the death penalty. In that case I would have likely been executed by now, and I wouldn't be writing this book. My story would have ended right there.

But my story didn't end there. In fact, it had only just begun.

CHAPTER 2
Black Monday
October 19, 1987

DURING COLORADO'S INDIAN SUMMER, warm weather lingers as blue autumn skies grace the Rocky Mountains, and stunning colors accent the crisp, clean mountain air. The morning of October 19, 1987, was the beginning of just such a perfect Chamber of Commerce day in the Rockies.

Wall Street investors remember October 19, 1987, as "Black Monday." On that day, the Dow Jones Industrial Average dropped 500 points as stunned traders and panicked investors watched their fortunes disintegrate. October 19, 1987, was a day of reckoning for me as well. On that spectacular Colorado morning, I appeared before Chief District Court Judge Donald Campbell for a little heart-to-heart about my night out with Elliot. Six months had passed since my arrest, and judgment day had finally arrived. The court was going to sentence me for my crimes.

During the six months following my arrest I had lived a pretty miserable life, even by my standards. Although I was free on bail, I didn't feel free at all. Anxiety twisted my stomach into knots. The anxiety was like the nervous feeling you get when something really scary is about to happen—only this anxiety lasted for six months, nonstop. I thought about running, maybe to Mexico or some other damn place. But doing that takes serious stones, and I didn't like the idea of looking over my shoulder for the rest of my life. So I stayed. And I waited. And I drank.

For those six months, no matter what I did, my mind was paralyzed by dread and fear. I leeched off my wife's waitressing money and justified my drinking as the only way to deal with the stress. It never occurred to me that my wife was going through an awful situation as well. I was too self-absorbed to see beyond my own desperate existence.

Even though I was tortured by fear, I didn't really grasp the magnitude of what I had done or how much trouble I was really in. I expected the world to sympathize with me. On my attorney's suggestion, I attended some rehab meetings so that I would be able to show the judge at sentencing that I was committed to changing my life. When my attorney asked me how the meetings were going, I told him they were great and that I was learning a lot about my drinking.

In reality, the meetings brought me down so low that I had to go out drinking afterward to boost my spirits. I felt I couldn't relate even remotely to the people I saw and heard in those meetings. They were pathetic and desperate—and I wasn't. No, not me! I kept telling myself that I was nothing like them, and after a couple of drinks, I actually believed it.

I finally figured out a way to avoid the meetings altogether. Instead of getting the meeting chairperson to sign my "sign-in" sheet as proof of my attendance, I simply forged the chairperson's signature. I quickly learned that if I wrote down the signatures while I was drunk, none of them looked alike. Then I convinced strangers at the bar to do the signing, which guaranteed a variety of signatures. I was so smart I could hardly stand myself.

As the sentencing date approached, my drinking got worse. You might think that because drinking was largely responsible for so much of the misery in my life, I might have considered slowing down. Not a chance. At the time, I hadn't even made the connection that drinking was the great cause of my misery. Instead, I remained paralyzed with fear and dread, all the while telling myself there was nothing to worry about. I spent my days obsessing about what would happen at the sentencing, and I managed my insanity with booze.

Even though I was oblivious to the reality of my situation, my wife understood how much trouble I was in and that drinking was a big part of the problem. She grew frustrated with my apparent lack of concern for her or anything else. During one argument she asked, "Obviously you don't give a shit about keeping this marriage together, but don't you give a shit about your own goddamn life?" It was a fair question. I had no answer.

As my sentencing neared, my lawyer told me that Elliot had pleaded guilty to one count of aggravated robbery and had been sentenced to sixteen years in prison. "Sixteen years?" I repeated, incredulous at the news. I did not believe it. I did not want to believe it. I could not believe it. It was not true. Maybe my lawyer had meant to say sixteen months. There was no way I could spend sixteen *days* in prison, much less sixteen years.

Elliot had indeed been sentenced to sixteen years, and for the first time I began to understand how deep in the shit I really was. I realized that despite a lifetime of bailing my ass out of trouble, my mommy and daddy would not be able to save me this time. My life was in the hands of the judge. I became more afraid than I had ever been in my life.

My fear subsided slightly when I learned that Elliot had a prior criminal record. I rationalized that because of his record and because he was the one who had fired the gun, the judge had given him a particularly harsh sentence. Certainly the judge would understand that I was just a harmless guy with no record who had had a little too much to drink and picked up the wrong hitchhiker. The judge couldn't think that I was as bad a person as Elliot, could he?

After consulting with my lawyer and worrying about what to do over those first few months, I accepted a plea bargain and pleaded guilty to one count of aggravated robbery, in exchange for a sentencing range of four to sixteen years with the possibility of probation. For the next several months I clung to the belief that I would probably get probation or some other sentence that didn't involve jail time. I had deluded myself into believing that I would never go to prison. Going to prison was so horrible that it just couldn't happen—especially to a first-time offender like me. I remembered as a kid driving past a prison when we went to my grandparents' house. Every time I saw it I wondered what it would be like to be stuck there. I imagined the horrible things that must happen inside.

I never considered that I was as responsible for the shooting as Elliot. Personal responsibility was a nonissue for me: I simply never accepted any. Sure, there was plenty of blame to go around—but none of it was mine.

October 19 arrived, and my father had flown in from Louisiana to lend me support. As we drove to the courthouse that morning, I nervously chitchatted about where we would go for lunch once this sentencing thing was over. My dad encouraged the conversation, perhaps out of pity for me, or perhaps because he was as delusional as I was about my prospects. I had robbed two men at gunpoint and nearly killed two others, and I was now facing anywhere from probation to sixteen years in prison; nevertheless, we were optimistic. Go figure.

We entered the courthouse, and I felt the building begin to close in around me. Everything seemed gray. The 1960s architecture, with its low, old ceilings, screamed, "Bureaucracy!" The courthouse was minimalist, governmental, and claustrophobic.

As we exited the elevator and worked our way to the courtroom, dread filled every cell in my body. While we remained in the hallway I knew I was safe, and I wanted the walk to the courtroom to take as long as possible. But we soon came to a large set of double doors. A small sign displayed the message "Quiet. Court in Session."

Next to the doors, a sheet of paper listed a series of cases under the heading "Docket." I quickly scanned the list and found my name. It was official. This was no dream. There was no mistake: Now was the time. Here was the place. I couldn't manage my own life, and the government was stepping in to manage it for me.

We silently entered the courtroom and took a seat on a hard, wooden bench. The bailiff said, "All rise," and the judge replied, "Be seated." My hearing was under way. Within moments my case was called, and I approached an old wooden lectern. My attorney stood beside me, and the sentencing commenced.

The emotional impact of being sentenced in criminal court is a special mixture of nausea, anxiety, and pure, unadulterated fear. Under such intense pressure, the mind sometimes plays silly little games to cope with the stress. My fantasy was that I was going to leave the courthouse through the same door I had entered, a free man.

During the sentencing, I actually lost touch with reality. Even in the days and weeks immediately following the sentencing, I could not remember the details. I suppose I was in a state of total denial—or shock.

I do have vague memories of the district attorney going on about what a piece of shit I was, although he used fancier words. Unlike other convicts who complain about the way prosecutors portrayed them, I recall that I agreed with much of what the DA said. The guy read me like a children's story. It was my defense attorney who seemed to be talking about somebody else.

To this day, I have no idea whether or not I said anything during the proceeding. Knowing me, I am sure I said something: I just can't recall what it was. My guess is that I begged like a spoiled child to be spared prison. I couldn't disagree with the DA's opinion of me, but prison seemed a little much.

Of course, the judge's opinion was the only one that mattered, and the judge did not see things the way I did. As he spoke, I began to feel as though my anxiety and fear might come up with my breakfast. Things were not looking good for the home team. In fact, things were bad and quickly getting worse.

I remember hearing something about being (me, not him) a danger to society or protecting (him, not me) society or something along those lines. As my head swam, I heard the words "remanded to the custody of the Colorado Department of Corrections for a period of ten . . ."

Have you ever noticed how your mind can think about things at lightning speed? Well, just as the judge said, "ten," I felt my knees buckle. My mind screamed, *Ten months! That's almost a year!*

It was at precisely that moment that the word *years* made its way into my consciousness. My ears must have been playing tricks on me. *All right,* I told myself, *what this robed man means is that if I ever do anything like this again (which I swear I won't), then I'm going to prison for ten years. But that's okay, because I swear on my life that there will never be a next time. From here on out, I'm on the straight and narrow. Because if I'm not, that man in the black dress is going to go through with this ten years in prison thing and that must* never *happen.*

It was all perfectly settled in my mind.

Two deputies approached me from behind. They each took one of my arms and began pushing my wrists together behind my back and placing some silver-looking metal devices around them. All I could think was, *Where did these two come from? Didn't they understand that the robed person meant I would go to prison for ten years if I did something like this* again? *And since I will never do anything like this again, there is no need for these silver things around my wrists.* It was all a misunderstanding. Hadn't they heard about my lunch plans with my father?

Now they were ushering me toward the wrong door. This was not the main door of the courtroom. This was not the door that I had entered through. They were pushing me toward the back door—the portal to hell.

As the deputies shoved me toward eternal damnation, I looked over at my shocked father and my ashen wife. They seemed as confused as I was. They just stood there in stunned silence, and I stared silently back at them. Family folklore has it that I went out of the courthouse screaming, "Dad, save me!" The reality was far less dramatic. I walked out of the courtroom silently. I didn't have the energy to resist.

After I passed through the doorway, I was guided down a typical hallway past pedestrian-looking offices, where demons that looked like normal people were doing their everyday jobs. These people went about their office work, oblivious to the cataclysmic event that had just transpired a few feet away. No one so much as looked up. Didn't they understand that the judge had just sentenced me to *ten years* in prison?

This was a big deal. I expected everyone to be talking excitedly about it. But no one was discussing my case. All I saw was a bunch of regular people going about their work—reading and filing, doing standard office tasks. The chaos and confusion and screaming in my brain contrasted sharply with the calm orderliness of the courthouse offices around me.

The two deputies led me to a small, empty room, where they removed my belt and tie. I knew this was for suicide prevention, and their confiscation of my clothing reinforced the desperation of my situation. We then continued our journey down the hall and into an elevator. We traveled down several floors and exited deep beneath the city streets, where I was escorted through a long, narrow corridor to the booking area, housed in this subterranean shithole. I answered a few perfunctory questions, trying hard not to let my voice betray the fear and helplessness I was feeling, and I was booked into county jail to begin serving my ten-year prison sentence.

It's funny how the word *ten* completely changed my life, yet for the deputy who processed me, it was just three tiny letters that made up one itsy-bitsy little word—a word to be typed on a document and sent along its bureaucratic way without a second thought. My life was over, yet the three letters that rendered it so were completely insignificant to anyone outside of my dysfunctional reality. The world kept right on spinning while my mind melted down. My insignificance and irrelevance frightened me. What I didn't realize then was that I was just another loser on his way to prison. There was nothing unique or special about me. I was just one of thousands of guys who had walked down the same hall, taken a ride down the same elevator, and stood in front of the same desk. What seemed like a huge deal to me was routine for everyone around me. Nothing personal, Mr. Long, just business as usual. When the deputies finished booking me, they handed me a brown paper bag containing my lunch. Just another day at the office.

I was placed in a holding cell in the booking area. The holding cell was a small concrete bunker about fifteen feet long and six feet wide, nestled deep underneath the courthouse in the bowels of the city. At one end of the room was a steel door with a small window in its center. Concrete benches lined the walls. A small drain in the center of the room served as a urinal. It was definitely hell.

Lunch turned out to be a piece of bologna on white bread, with a finger impression smashed right in the center of the bread, and a container of warm milk. It seemed the stories of bread and water were just rumors. But I had never imagined that real prison food would be bologna and warm milk. I wasn't hungry, so I gave my lunch to one of the five or six guys who were in the cell with me, waiting. This guy apparently had been there long enough to develop an appetite.

Someone laughed in the office next door. It was my father! I sighed in relief, realizing this whole thing was a joke to frighten me, worked out by the judge, my attorney, and my dear old dad, who was right next door, arranging for my imminent release. I sat there for an hour, believing in this fantasy, until it finally dawned on me that someone else had a laugh just like my dad's. For the first time in my life, I was beyond the help of my parents or anyone else. No one was going to get me out of this one.

There are no words to describe the loneliness, isolation, and fear I felt on that day, my personal Black Monday. I had no idea what to expect next. I had no idea where I was going and for how many years I might be there. I had no idea whether I would ever see my family again. I had no idea how my life had degenerated to this point.

I had never really had a plan for my life, but somehow I thought things would just work out. I was wrong. Life simply doesn't work that way. Successful lives are not the result of luck. "Destiny," I once read, "is a matter of choice, not a matter of chance."

I had been at a crossroads that night in the parking lot with Elliot. I could have chosen either path, but I chose the path of least resistance and maximum pain. It's amazing how much pain we will endure before we choose to do something about it. And I hadn't even begun to scratch pain's surface.

I began to wait—for what I don't know. But I waited for hours. Then days. Then weeks. During that time, I had plenty of time to think back over my life and how I had gotten to this awful place.

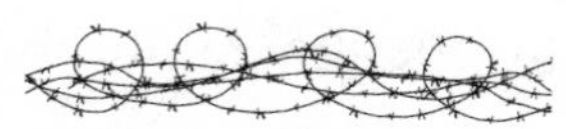

CHAPTER 3
Me
1964 to 1987

I WAS BORN ON JANUARY 18, 1964, in Paris. Not that Paris, the other one . . . in Arkansas. I was the youngest of five children. Named after both Grandfathers, Weldon Willard quickly became "Wally."

My dad, Richard Long, was a career military man, which means that he always had a job, but he never had any money. I sensed that my dad was unhappy with his lot in life. I think he would have preferred to live a much different life—one that didn't include a wife and five hungry mouths to feed and, worse yet, listen to.

He always acted as if he was at the mercy of something, although I couldn't tell you what that thing was. I don't think he ever once imagined that his life could have been different. Better. He never understood that he did indeed have a choice about how he would live. In his mind his life could only be one thing—a life of misery—and by God, he would take it like a man. My father was many things, but a whiner he was not.

He was, however, a drinker.

For the most part my dad was a happy drunk. In fact, I learned at a young age that the best time to ask him for anything was after a little Seagram's V.O. Canadian whiskey had helped adjust his attitude. Though my father was emotionally disconnected from his family, he was never abusive. He just didn't like his life, and drinking was his way of making things a little less miserable.

I respected and loved my father, although I emulated his bad habits more than his good ones. My dad could stretch a dollar forever, and my parents always paid their bills on time, yet I was completely irresponsible with money and had destroyed my credit by the time I was twenty. My dad always worked and held a job, but I became a deadbeat. Unfortunately, drinking was the one habit that I inherited.

While my father turned to the bottle, my mother turned to the Jehovah's Witnesses. She used religion as a tonic to cope with her difficulties. I fully appreciate the positive impact that religion has had on my mother and so many others, and eventually, developing a spiritual life became an important element of my own salvation. However, Jehovah's Witnesses view themselves as completely separate from the world. In accordance with church practices, my mother referred to anything outside the organization as "worldly." I can remember as a youngster thinking that the "world" was a very bad place and that "worldly" people could not be trusted.

My dad's military career required us to move a lot. In those days it wasn't unusual for a military family to move every year or two. In fact, the first time I started a school year with kids I knew from the year before was in the ninth grade; prior to that I was in a new school with new faces every year. I was envious of the kids who had friends they had known for years. I never developed that sense of community. I was always the outsider.

The combination of having an emotionally disconnected, alcoholic father, being forced into a religion that warned me to eschew and distrust society, and moving almost every year eventually destroyed my self-esteem. I grew to be an insecure, neurotic, and isolated teenager who felt no connection with anyone and saw no place for himself in the world.

Alcohol changed all that—or at least it changed my self-image. Looking back, I can understand why my father drank to make his life more bearable. I did exactly the same thing.

I remember with surprising clarity the first time alcohol "improved" my life. I was fourteen years old and had snuck out to a bonfire with my friend Keith and some evil "worldly" kids from school. Keith was the coolest guy I had ever met. I idolized him. He was handsome and very popular, especially with the girls. Keith also came from a Jehovah's Witnesses family, but unlike me, he came from a family with stable roots in the community. I admired the fact that Keith always seemed confident and comfortable in his own skin. He always seemed to belong. He was Danny Zuko from *Grease*. I was the exact opposite.

As I stood around the fire that night, watching everyone laugh, talk, and enjoy themselves, I felt as though I was on the outside, looking in. I had no connection with the crowd. I felt alone. Feeling awkward and out of place, I grabbed a Miller pony from a cooler. After I knocked back the beer, it didn't take long before I began to understand why my father drank. It felt good. I drank another, and things felt even better.

Before I knew it, I was part of the scene—laughing, talking, and joking with my peers. I felt confident and connected. I fit in. I was part of the group, and it was awesome. I felt better than I ever had in my life. From that night forward, beer was my friend—the Great Elixir, my social lubrication, my wonderful, life-giving, confidence-building Beer. Now, I would have a wonderful life, just like everyone else.

Within a year I had dropped out of school and greeted the world with a ninth-grade education and no marketable skills.

But I had beer, and beer was good.

Even though I was a fifteen-year-old kid with no prospects, I remained optimistic about my future. It seems preposterous, of course, given my circumstances, yet something inside me remained ambitious and hopeful. I'd always had big dreams, but I was unwilling to make the sacrifices that successful people seemed to be willing to make. I was also very short on persistence—a quality vital for success. Whenever I got something going in my life that was healthy or positive, I always gave it up the second the going got tough. I wanted the fruits of success, but I was never willing to grow the tree.

Still, I had hope. When I was fifteen, I decided that I would make a fortune purchasing wholesale auto parts and reselling them to gas stations and mechanic shops. I somehow managed to convince my father to give me a few thousand dollars to start my business. I was unwilling to work a job to get the start-up money. It was much easier to badger my dad for it.

I don't know why my father agreed to give me the money. Most likely he knew that I wouldn't succeed but acted out of guilt and pity for his pathetic son. I took his money and drove to a parts warehouse, where I purchased several boxes of fan belts, radiator hoses, and fuses, loaded them in the back of my father's pickup, and drove off.

Selling auto parts out of boxes in the back of a pickup to gas stations and mechanics turned out to be more difficult than I had expected. It seemed the gas stations and mechanic shops already had suppliers and they were buying supplies at the same prices I was paying. The fact that I was fifteen years old probably didn't improve my chances of success. So I gave up after about a week. It was a behavioral pattern that I would repeat many times in my life as I tried, and failed, at a variety of get-rich-quick schemes. I was unwilling to do any real work and gave up at the slightest hint of resistance.

So I persisted in looking for the easy way in all things. I even got married in 1984, looking for an easy relationship with an innocent seventeen-year-old girl. In 1985, I was twenty-one years old and decided to open a business selling and installing automotive accessories. I figured I needed about twenty-five grand to get the business rolling and have a little "cushion." Since I had already trashed my credit, I turned to dear old Dad, who apparently had learned nothing about the hazards of lending me money from my earlier auto parts fiasco.

With my mother's help I convinced (read: manipulated) my father into getting a loan for me, and I set out once again to build an empire. Unfortunately, empires are difficult to build and require a lot of work and sacrifice. As you might have guessed, these were not my strong suits.

In January 1986, with my father's borrowed money, I opened a company called ARTCAR on Veterans Boulevard, a six-lane highway just outside New Orleans. Initially things went great. We quickly became the largest business of our type in the city. But then a strange thing happened: suppliers wanted to get paid. Some even downright expected to get paid. And so did the federal and state governments.

After six or eight months my accountant informed me that I had a tax problem. I routinely withheld payroll taxes from employees' checks but didn't bother to send that money to the state revenue department or the IRS. And I had a tendency to use the company's revenue as a personal piggy bank, spending money faster than it came in.

By the fall of 1986, the company was in serious financial trouble, and the writing was on the wall. Suppliers were cutting us off. The

IRS was sending nasty letters. I had managed to destroy the business and spend all of the loan money, all within nine or ten months.

After the business imploded, I packed my wife and everything we owned, which wasn't much, into a pickup and a U-Haul trailer and fled to Colorado. We arrived in Denver in January 1987.

There, I did nothing but drink, while my wife worked in an effort to salvage some piece of a normal life. She didn't stand a chance. I think she figured out pretty early on in our marriage that I wasn't going to amount to much, yet she hung in there while I did my best to destroy my life and hers. I remember her as mentally tough and independent, although looking back, I realize I never really knew her at all. I can only surmise that it was her pride and self-reliance that kept her from going back to her parents before I completely disintegrated, doing everything in my power to take her down with me.

Finally, on May 12, 1987, I surrendered to the force I had pretended to fight for so many years. It had really been no fight at all. I was never really in the match. I had given up years before but had deluded myself into believing that the outcome might somehow be different. I jumped over the line that separated light from darkness, good from evil.

I pulled the truck over and asked the hitchhiker if he needed a ride. "Sure," Elliot said, and we drove off, unaware of what the night would bring.

CHAPTER 4

I'm Going to Cañon City, Cañon City Here I Come . . .

December 1987 to Spring 1990

IN DECEMBER 1987, AFTER WAITING around for two months in the El Paso County Jail, I was transferred to the Colorado Department of Corrections Reception and Diagnostic Unit in Cañon City, Colorado. Within moments of my arrival, I decided the word *reception* was totally false advertising.

Located about two hours south of Denver, Cañon City is as "Old West" as you'll find in Colorado: a small town founded as a farming and ranching community, surrounded by stunning mountains. The charm of the town contrasts sharply with the misery and desperation that live behind the stone walls of the state prison.

The prison industry came to Cañon City over a hundred years ago when convict labor constructed the Colorado Territorial Correctional Facility from limestone blocks quarried from the surrounding hills. Today the Colorado Department of Corrections and the Federal Bureau of Prisons are the largest employers in Fremont County. Cañon City is home to the state's prison museum (yes, they really have one). It's a prison town, and if a resident doesn't work at one of the prisons, it's a safe bet that he or she knows someone who does.

The original facility, known as "Old Max," is still in use, although a newer prison with modern architecture and security now serves as Colorado's maximum-security prison. Old Max once housed some of the Old West's most notorious criminals, such as Alfred Packer, who was convicted of murdering and eating five companions on a prospecting expedition in 1874. Now known as "the Walls" by the inmates who live there, the facility was once the site of Colorado's gas chamber, located just above death row.

The stone walls that surround the Walls are forty feet high, marked with gun towers housing armed guards in mirrored sunglasses to monitor the activity below. When I stepped off the bus before these giant walls I felt as if I was stepping back in time. The facility was almost a perfect caricature of what a prison should look like. I was scared and intimidated. I wanted to go home.

Instead, shackled with belly chains, handcuffs, and ankle chains, I shuffled through an entryway into a low-ceilinged waiting room in the "reception" unit, also known as Cell House #5. I was told to take a seat on one of the wooden benches set against the walls and wait. Eventually I was assigned a Department of Corrections inmate number—57676—and given a brief orientation from a guy everyone called Lurch, as in Lurch from *The Addams Family.* His resemblance to the TV character was uncanny. In a monosyllabic monotone, Lurch threatened, "Your ass is mine. I'm not your 'mutha.'" (Wow! Almost two syllables.) "You don't have shit comin' to you." It all seemed straightforward enough.

Legend had it that Lurch had once been a high-ranking officer in the prison food chain, but he'd been busted down a notch or two for knocking the snot out of inmates. Based on my initial impression of him, the story seemed plausible. Lurch struck me as the kind of guy who valued cop-on-inmate violence far more than reaching professional milestones. I later learned that since most of the surrounding area is farm and ranch country, many of the prison guards are cowboys at heart. I have no problem with cowboys, but as a general rule, cowboys are not big fans of convicts. Enough said.

For the next several hours I waited on a wooden bench and talked with other convicts. Most everyone I talked to had been through the system before, so I tried to get as much information as I could about what to expect over the next ten years. I learned very quickly that it was unlikely I would serve a full sentence—I would probably be back on the street in four or five. It still seemed like a long time.

Eventually I was given some bedding material, a bar of soap, and a cell assignment and was told to walk up two flights of stairs to the top tier of the cell house. As I made my way down the tier, I looked over the handrail to my right. *If I jump and land on my head*, I thought, *I could end it all right here and now*. But it was only about a twenty-five-foot fall to the ground floor. There was a good chance I might only suffer brain damage or paralysis, making a bad situation even worse.

On my left was an endless row of bars separating me from some angry-looking people, who were taunting me with shouts of, "Fresh meat!" I breathed deep in an effort to keep my cool, but inside I was crying like a little girl.

I had walked almost to the end of the tier when a cell door opened on my left. A voice over the loudspeaker told me to step inside. I quickly obeyed and heard the door clang shut behind me.

I was officially in state prison.

Over the next couple of weeks I took a battery of diagnostic tests. I scored about 100 on the IQ test and did pretty well on the academic material, considering that I was a high school dropout. Where I really excelled, however, was on the needs assessment for alcohol and drug treatment. Everybody is good at something, right?

For a couple of hours each day I was allowed to go outside to a small asphalt yard, which was surrounded by the forty-foot stone walls and guard towers. It wasn't much, but after two months in county jail it was nice to be outside—even if it was December in Colorado.

Three times a day a loud bell would ring, signaling it was time to make the two-hundred-yard walk into the main part of the prison for chow. Each time the bell rang, my cell door would slide open for a few seconds and I would step onto the tier and make the walk to the chow hall. The door would slide shut quickly, so if I wasn't ready to go, there would be no chow. You snooze, you lose. Many times I would ignore the early morning bell for breakfast and try to sleep as long as I could. I always thought, *The more hours I spend sleeping, the fewer hours I have to spend awake*. It didn't feel like serving time while I slept.

Each evening the inmate trustees, called "Tier Queers," turned on the showers at the end of the tier, and the guards opened six or eight cell doors at a time for community showers. Being vulnerable is a staple of prison life, but walking the tier past twenty cells in only a skimpy towel was always a little unnerving. Bumping against naked men as you washed your ass added even more uncertainty to the situation.

Prison life would take a lot of getting used to.

The highlight of my stay in Cell House #5 was a visit from my wife and her sister. Visits in prison are proof that you're still alive. They are a light shining under a door in a pitch-black room. They are a gasp of air when you are buried alive. Visits are a welcome break from the insanity, as long as prisoners and wives remember to play by two simple rules.

Rule #1: All parties must not mention the fact that the prisoner will be locked up for many years.

Rule #2: All parties must not mention the fact that eventually the wife's visits will end.

Few women bargain for the shame and humiliation that comes with having a husband in prison. At some point, most wives will pick up the pieces of their lives and take up with someone new. It's unreasonable and unfair to expect otherwise.

Circumstances create the rules. Human nature ensures their inevitability. At the end of visiting hours, reality creeps back in as the wife returns to the real world and the prisoner returns to the surreal world of prison life. The prisoner never knows when the final visit will come.

I spent Christmas of 1987 on death row. Fortunately for me, it was Colorado's old death row located in Cell House #3. I was housed in this unit after I completed my diagnostic testing, while I waited to be transferred to a permanent facility.

Just above the cellblock where I was housed was the old gas chamber, which was now used for Bible study and twelve-step programs. I never went up there. I was not going to be one of those guys who came to prison and found God. And I certainly didn't have a drinking problem, so there was nothing up there for me besides an old gas chamber, which I had no desire to see.

I remember that December being bitterly cold. The heaters didn't work well in the old stone building. When it got really cold outside, you could see your breath inside. Ice formed on the inside of the windows that were about twenty-five feet across from my cell. It was hard to stay warm. I remember thinking that a man could die if left exposed to the bitter temperatures. A man's spirit could also die if left exposed to the loneliness of life in prison.

A few weeks later, in January 1988, I was transferred to Buena Vista Correctional Facility (BVCF) in the heart of the central Rockies. Built in the 1800s, the facility was located just to the west of Mounts Harvard, Yale, Princeton, and Oxford, four of Colorado's most scenic "fourteeners," or mountains over 14,000 feet tall. The majesty of these spectacular peaks contrasted with the misery and desperation at their feet.

Originally constructed as a reformatory, BVCF was now a medium-security prison. The prison was called the "Gladiator School" because it was home to many young men doing serious prison time who were determined to make names for themselves within the Colorado prison system. I didn't share their ambition, but I did share their home at BVCF for the next year.

My cell at "Bueny," as the prison was called, was just like the cells in the movies. A metal bunk with a skinny foam mattress lined the left side of the six-by-ten-foot cell. At the head of the bunk there was a small metal desk bolted to the cement floor, with an attached metal stool that swiveled out. Midway down the right-hand wall was a small stainless steel toilet and sink, designed as one self-contained unit so the sink drained into the toilet.

Welcome home, Wally. Welcome home, I thought.

Gradually I grew accustomed to my life behind bars. Things that were insignificant in the real world took on new importance. Making phone calls to home or preparing a burrito from goods purchased at the prison canteen were events to be anticipated and relished. Keeping my tennis shoes white and clean and ironing my prison greens (uniforms) for visits became ridiculously critical tasks. When you have no control over significant things, control over insignificant details takes on an exaggerated importance. But I was beginning to get comfortable, and that was a dangerous thing. A healthy fear of prison is the only thing that keeps some men from coming back—getting comfortable makes it easier to return.

During that first year, my wife continued to visit, making the two-hour drive from Denver almost every weekend. But the strain on her was beginning to show. The fear, the loneliness, and the frustration of prison life affected her as much as it affected me. I waited and wondered and hoped for a miracle, but deep down I knew. It was only a matter of time before the visits ended.

Near the end of 1988, after I'd been incarcerated for a little over a year, the sentencing court notified me that the judge had granted a hearing for a "Motion for Reconsideration." At this hearing, the court would review my sentence to determine whether any modification was warranted.

According to conventional prison wisdom, if a judge went through all the trouble to transfer me back to court to reconsider my case, he was probably willing to adjust the sentence. If the judge didn't want to modify my sentence, he could simply deny the motion to reconsider without transferring me back to court. At the hearing, the judge might reduce my sentence or even resentence me to probation. I had heard that sometimes a judge used so-called "shock incarceration" to give first-time offenders a scare. My wife and I were very excited. We were sure the initial harsh sentence was only a warning. I was going to have that lunch with my family after all—maybe a year late, but better late than never.

As the reconsideration date drew near, the visits with my wife became less strained. There was finally a light at the end of the tunnel. I would be home soon, and this nightmare would be over. I would get a job and start a new life. No more wasting time. No more stupid stunts. No more drinking. No more prison. This was my big chance.

Finally, the hearing date arrived, and I was transported back to Colorado Springs, about two hours from Bueny. As I waited in a holding cell several stories beneath the courthouse, I realized the whole experience had served a purpose. I had learned some important lessons that would no doubt make me a more responsible, mature adult. I was okay with all that had happened.

A deputy escorted me into the courtroom. I saw my wife sitting in the gallery. She looked hopeful and relieved. It had been a horrific year, but it was finally over. Maybe the time away had done me some good.

As the judge began to review my file, I felt confident. My lawyer had told me that even if the judge did not resentence me to probation, there was a good chance he would place me in a work-release program in which I could earn some money and spend some time at home with my wife. Work release was an excellent alternative to no release.

Finally, the judge began to speak. I was happy to hear him acknowledge that since I was a first-time offender and because I had behaved myself during my year in prison an adjustment in my sentence was, indeed, justified. "Therefore," the judge said, "motion to reconsider is granted, and the defendant's sentence is hereby reduced by two years."

As in my first sentencing, I thought for a moment that the judge had made a mistake. He had reduced my sentence by two years. That couldn't be right. That meant I still had an eight-year sentence to serve. But I had heard correctly. I still had a long prison term ahead of me. I stood in stunned disbelief, just as I had a year earlier. And just as had happened a year earlier, two deputies escorted me out the wrong door.

Immediately following my return to Buena Vista, my case manager called with some good news. He told me that the two-year reduction in my sentence meant that I would be eligible for a reduction in my security classification. I would be going to a minimum-security prison located on the western slope of Colorado. This was, indeed, good news. Maybe I wasn't going home, but I was going to an "honor camp."

Within a week or so I was transferred to the Rifle Correctional Center, located about an hour west of Vail, Colorado, just off Interstate 70. There were no fences and no cellblocks—only dormitory-style housing units. The facility grounds were situated above the Rifle Gap Reservoir, a popular camping and fishing area. It was a welcome change from real prison.

After a couple of weeks at this new, less secure facility, things began to look better. I learned that with my sentence reduction I would be eligible for work-release placement within two years. With one year of prison under my belt, I was making progress.

I began to jog on a regular basis. The warden even allowed inmates to run down to the reservoir twice a week as part of a mental health program. Moreover, I learned that all the inmates were allowed to travel into the town of Rifle and attend classes at Colorado Mountain College, a small community college. It was hard to believe this was actually prison. We were even allowed to wear civilian clothes.

Visits in this facility were much better as well. Instead of the strict rules of a prison visiting room, I now had visits at a picnic table next to a barbecue grill. Visitors were even permitted to bring picnic supplies into the visiting facility. Before long I was enjoying steak and baked potatoes during visits with my wife. I began to think maybe things would be okay; maybe we would somehow make it through this nightmare.

Then the inevitable happened. One day in the spring of 1989, my wife came to visit. Following our little picnic she informed me that she wouldn't be coming to see me anymore. This would be her last visit. She didn't tell me at the time, but I knew what had happened. She had met someone else.

I really hadn't seen it coming. I tried to talk her out of it. She was casual and direct about her feelings. There was no changing her mind. I called her several times afterward, but deep down I understood that this was how it had to end.

We had married when we were very young, and she had never signed on for this kind of life. She expected more from me, and she was ultimately unable to overcome her disappointment and disillusion with who I really was. Despite feeling hurt and confused, I knew I had brought this on myself, and I respected and appreciated her directness. Many women would have lied in a similar situation, yet she had the integrity to be honest rather than leading me to believe our relationship was something it was not. She had done the best she could, but the reality that I would be gone for at least two more years was the last straw.

Within a few months we were divorced. That was the end of my first marriage.

To distance myself from my personal problems, and because I had previously earned my GED, I decided to attend Colorado Mountain College.

It was a small school, with no more than one hundred students in the entire college at any given time. Everybody knew who the inmates were. While we weren't supposed to fraternize with other students, inmates were permitted to interact with other students during class sessions, and some of the guys had developed relationships with local girls. I had read once that many women are attracted to reformed "bad boys." This seemed to be the case in Rifle, where a number of women had a strange fascination with their convict classmates. Unfortunately, most of us "bad boys" hadn't done much reforming. These budding romances didn't stand a chance.

I met a girl during my second semester. Though we had flirted some during classes, I really didn't see the relationship going anywhere. She was, after all, married with three kids. This was quite a track record for a twenty-one-year-old girl, but she seemed nice enough.

Just before the semester break she gave me her phone number and said I could call her during the time off. Back in those days, the phones at Rifle were regular pay phones, and we could call whomever we chose with quarters purchased at the canteen. It was almost like real college.

I started calling her every day. We talked for hours while her husband worked to support her and her three kids. If I'd had even an ounce of decency I would have nixed the relationship, but I was twenty-five years old and desperate for attention, especially so soon after my wife had dumped me. The impact that my flirtations might have on her family was inconsequential to me. I wasn't interested in who might get hurt. I was only interested in me. I was a punk, and that's how punks think and behave.

Over the next year I attended classes at Colorado Mountain College and met surreptitiously with my new friend around the small campus. I interspersed our meetings with regular phone calls to her home. She had convinced her husband that I was just a classmate with whom she was working on school projects. I never knew whether he was aware that I was a convict from the local prison.

Once the sting of my divorce began to wear off, I started to focus on getting an education. I became obsessed with making high grades. I was in some kind of competition with myself to prove I wasn't a thief and a criminal, even though I was slithering around with a married woman. Ignoring the potential consequences, I took enormous risks to facilitate this relationship. We met between classes in her friend's camper, which had been conveniently left unlocked in the college parking lot. We were a real class act.

I was unable to be honest with myself or others about my past. I pretended that I had had a successful life before prison and that my criminal act was an aberration. I avoided conversations with myself about the crime I had committed. I had brief thoughts about it, but there was no real introspection or self-examination—I never thought about who I was and the criminal things I had done. I was exactly where I belonged, yet I believed I was somehow different from the other felons. I was oblivious to my own hypocrisy when I told myself I was a good person who would never come back to prison, while I simultaneously carried on with a married woman who had three kids.

In the spring of 1990 I learned I would be conditionally released to a halfway house in Colorado Springs. After serving less than three years of my eight-year sentence, I would be released to make a go of my life once again. Despite having the opportunity—and three years' time—to examine my life and deal with the self-absorption that motivated my behavior, I left prison unable to accept who and what I really was and unprepared to lead an honorable, responsible life.

Society would pay a heavy price for my lack of introspection.

CHAPTER 5

Back on the Street Again

Spring 1990 to December 1, 1991

IN THE SPRING OF 1990, I entered a work-release program in Colorado Springs. The Community Corrections program, known as Com-Cor, was designed to help convicts manage the transition from prison to parole and eventual release.

The halfway house facility was housed in what was once a small roadside motel in the old north end of Colorado Springs. Each room accommodated six to eight convicts, all of whom had been recently released from prison. While the rooms were cramped with too many residents and too many bunk beds, the opportunity to get a job and live in the community was a welcome relief from real prison life; nevertheless, residents living there were still technically in the Department of Corrections and could be sent back to the joint on a moment's notice.

While Rifle was a minimum-security prison and I was allowed to attend college classes under prison supervision, the halfway house was almost like being on the streets. I would be free to work and live in the community, as long as I was back at the halfway house by the 11:00 PM curfew.

My case manager was a blond, curly-headed man named Jarle (pronounced: yar-ly) Wood, who looked more like a California surfer dude than a prison counselor. Jarle was soft-spoken yet disturbingly direct. "I'll give you plenty of rope while you're here, Mr. Long," he said. "You'll either hang yourself or you won't." His rehabilitation philosophy seemed simple enough, but I wondered how simple it would be for me to follow.

Not long after arriving at Com-Cor, I found a job working for a small business doing pin-striping and window tinting on cars. I began working—and waiting for whatever was to come next. I had no plan, other than never returning to prison.

My girlfriend from Rifle regularly made the four-hour drive to see me in Colorado Springs, despite the inconvenience of juggling a husband and three kids. She told her husband that I was a "sick friend" in Colorado Springs, and he chose to ignore our budding relationship.

During this time I had one brief phone conversation with my ex-wife, and I arranged to retrieve the personal property that she had been holding for me over the past three years. She agreed to leave the items on her doorstep, and my new girlfriend picked them up as she passed through Denver on one of her trips to see me.

All that was left of my pre-prison life with my ex-wife was an old milk crate containing some pictures, a worn-out, empty wallet, and one shoe. I wanted to believe that my life was more than the sum of these random items, but the single shoe was a perfect metaphor for my pathetic life.

Within a few months, my girlfriend left her husband and moved herself and her three children to Colorado Springs; her husband had figured out that I was something more than a sick friend. The "plan" was for her to divorce him and then rely on me to support her and her kids. It didn't seem to register with her—or me—that I had never developed the ability to take responsibility for my own life, much less anyone else's. Yet there we were, playing house like adults.

Although I stayed busy with my new "life" over the next few months, I continued to have nagging thoughts about who and what I really was. I went to work each day, tried to take care of my new family, and even enrolled at the University of Colorado at Colorado Springs to build on the associate's degree I had earned at Colorado Mountain College in Rifle. But somehow my position never felt authentic. I always seemed to be playing a role in someone else's life. I was going through the motions, but I felt as if I was covered with a cheap paint job and that my true colors would eventually seep through.

I felt most out of place on campus. While I tried to convince myself that I was just like all the other students, I knew it wasn't true. I was pretending to be someone I was not. Deep down I knew I didn't belong. They were happy and confident; I was a convict and a criminal.

I was still the piece of shit that had held a gun on two innocent strangers in a dark, cold parking lot. I felt that if others were to learn the truth about me, they would keep their distance, stare, and talk in hushed tones about the filth that was trying desperately to be one of them. I was an interloper who had invaded their happy, normal college world. And the longer I remained among them, the more convinced I became that my fraud would be exposed. I felt pretty much as I had my entire life—like an outsider looking in.

I managed to keep things together long enough to complete one semester, but by then I could no longer play the joint roles of college student and responsible family man. The ultimate con in life is the one we play on ourselves. It was very confusing being both the mark and the con. I decided to acknowledge who I really was and bring the inauthentic act to an end.

So one evening, I walked into the campus lounge, slammed a few Coors Lights, and drove back to the halfway house. There, I took the breathalyzer test that was administered to all work-release inmates each time we returned to the facility. The corrections technician on duty watched as the digital reading climbed from 0.0 to 0.06.

He looked at me and asked, "Long, you been drinking?"

I looked at him and mumbled, "I guess. What does it say?"

"It says you've been drinking, is what it says."

"Well," I responded, "I guess I've been drinking then."

Blowing "hot" for booze resulted in an automatic "total grounds" restriction, meaning no work, no passes to go home, no nothing. Moreover, it very likely meant a trip back to the joint. I had downed the beers to shatter the pretense of my existence, but now I asked myself, *What in the hell am I doing?*

Was this what I wanted? Was this my response to the pressures of living a "normal" life? Was this my surefire way to get back to what I really was? Was this my way of ending the charade?

The tech ordered me to park my car and return the keys to the office. As I walked outside to move my car from the driveway to a parking spot, I realized that I would get hit with a conviction for driving under the influence. Coming back to the halfway house intoxicated was bad enough, but driving back to the halfway house while intoxicated was a more serious offense. After all, even a civilian living on the streets would go to jail if a cop caught him driving while impaired, yet here I was, a convict on conditional release from prison, living in a halfway house, and somehow I had not yet been arrested for driving under the influence. *All in good time*, I thought. In fact, I imagined that the technician was already on the phone with the police department, orchestrating my arrest for DUI.

I returned to the office and handed my keys to the technician. "Sit down and wait right there until you can provide," he told me.

Provide was a euphemism for providing a urine sample that would be sent for testing to confirm the breathalyzer results.

Within a few minutes, word had spread throughout the facility that someone had been busted. As I waited, the other inmates walked by and gave me looks that said, "Better you than me, asshole." I was the rule-breaking zoo animal, on display for everyone's entertainment. And everyone wanted—needed—to stare at me to gain the feeling of superiority that comes from not being the one on his way back to jail.

Some inmates feigned compassion in order to get the details about my implosion. "You okay, man? What happened?" they asked with mock concern.

"Go fuck yourself," I responded. I wasn't about to whine to them with my sob story so that they could revel in the details of my plight.

Others asked, "What do you want us to do with your property?" It was a rhetorical question. Correctional technicians always boxed up the personal property of anyone being "regressed" back to county jail, but by the time the techs got around to doing that, convicts had picked through all the goods and taken what they wanted.

Who gives a shit, right? I thought to myself. Wasn't this what I had expected when I decided that the pressure of playing by the rules was too much for me?

As I sat there, I listened for the call to the police department announcing my DUI. When I couldn't handle the suspense any longer, I asked the tech, "Am I going to jail or what?"

"I don't know," he responded. "It's up to your case manager."

My case manager was still Jarle Wood, the surfer dude turned cop. Jarle wasn't really a cop, of course, but in my prison world there were only cops and convicts. Just as he had warned, he had given me enough rope to hang myself. I figured that guys like me must be pretty predictable. I wondered how many others had hung themselves with the rope of opportunity that Jarle had given them.

After a while, I was finally ready to "provide." As I pissed in the cup I chuckled with the irony that I really was pissing away my life. The strange thing was that I didn't care. For a moment I could hear my ex-wife saying, "Don't you give a shit about your own goddamn life?"

When I handed the specimen cup to the tech, he told me to return to my room. I looked at him in disbelief. This could only mean that he had talked to Jarle, and Jarle had decided that I wasn't going to jail for DUI—at least not yet. As I returned to my room, I walked past my car and thought, *The tech didn't even mention that I drove in here and blew 0.06 into the machine.* I couldn't believe it.

The next morning I listened for the inevitable call over the PA system that would order me to report to my case manager's office. I was on "total grounds," so I couldn't leave the premises for any reason, even work. So I waited.

As I thought about the previous night, I wondered what was wrong with me. Why was I so intent on my own destruction? Why couldn't I take advantage of the opportunity to put prison and my past life behind me? The thoughts nagged at me, yet they were distant. They were more like an itch than the two-by-four wallop to the head that I needed to force a change in my behavior.

Finally the call came over the loudspeaker: "Weldon Long report to case manager's office."

I walked across the parking lot and down a flight of stairs to Jarle's basement office. Jarle shuffled some papers on his desk, hardly acknowledging my presence when I walked in. After a few moments he looked up, smiled, and said, "Morning. I heard you had some trouble last night." I could tell by the tone of his voice that this was just standard work for Jarle. Whether I went back to prison or not didn't matter to him. He would be going home to his family that night either way. Suddenly, I didn't want to go back to prison.

"Yeah, I guess so," I responded meekly.

"Here's your write-up for the hot breathalyzer," he said as he handed me some papers. "You'll have a DOC [Department of Corrections] hearing in a week or so, and a decision about whether or not you go back to prison will be made at that time. In the meantime you are on work only status. Any questions?"

"No," I responded.

"Okay," Jarle said. "By the way, your driving privileges are suspended as well."

"I understand," I mumbled as I turned and walked up the stairs and out of his office.

Jarle hadn't mentioned that I had been driving under the influence, except that I wouldn't be doing any more of it. Quickly, I went to the front office, signed out for work, and jumped on the transit bus. *Let someone else do the driving*, I thought as I headed downtown.

A week or so later, at my DOC hearing, I pleaded guilty to having a positive breathalyzer test. I lost my driving privileges and my recreational passes, but I was allowed to stay at the halfway house and keep my job. I wasn't going back to prison. The news that I would be staying didn't surprise me. If they had planned to send me back to the joint I would have been waiting for the DOC hearing in the county jail—not at the halfway house where I could have easily split. I viewed the incident as yet another lessoned learned, even though I hadn't truly learned anything.

Over the summer and fall I stayed out of trouble and regained my driving and pass privileges. The secret to my success was that I had learned how to drink without getting caught. Successful drinking depended on what I called the "magic ratio."

The magic ratio was simple: it took one and a half hours for each beer I drank to go through my system. But there was one caveat: the ratio was only effective after I had finished my last beer. Each time I had a pass to leave the halfway house, I used the ratio to determine how much I could drink and when I should stop drinking. If I had to be back at the facility by 11:00 PM, I could have four beers, as long as I finished them at least six hours before my return time. On a twelve-hour Sunday pass, I could drink six beers, as long as I finished them with at least nine hours remaining on pass.

My calculations worked beautifully; the magic ratio was my trusted friend. But there were two small problems. First, after drinking five or six beers, I tended to stretch my policy. So if I consumed six beers in the first two hours of a twelve-hour pass, I had ten hours remaining when I only needed nine to achieve an alcohol-free body. This seemed like a complete waste of an hour, so I often drank another beer.

Of course, this strategy put the whole calculation at risk, but I figured if my body could burn six beers in nine hours, it could probably handle eliminating seven beers in ten hours. This didn't abide by the magic ratio, but I rationalized that it was close enough for government work.

The ratio got considerably more complicated, however, on shorter passes. Passes after work, for instance, might last from only 6:00 PM to 11:00 PM. So, I could have two beers as long as I finished them by 8:00 PM, giving my body three hours to rid itself of the alcohol. But what if I consumed three beers by 7:00 PM? Could my body burn through three beers in four hours? How about four beers in five hours? As the beers flowed, the margin for error became smaller and smaller.

The second problem with the magic ratio was that it was rendered useless if the field accountability officer paid me an unexpected visit during a pass. No magic ratio was going to help me when that officer arrived on my doorstep, breathalyzer in hand.

While there was a probability of such a visit, it was not high, for my field accountability officer was a person of significant girth. He must have weighed nearly three hundred pounds. Now this fact alone would not have decreased the probability of my receiving a sobriety check, but when combined with the fact that the officer drove a small car, the odds of him walking up to my doorstep to administer a breathalyzer test dropped drastically.

Because my field accountability officer had a difficult time getting in and out of his car, his checks consisted of pulling up to the curb and calling me from his cell phone to ask that I stick my head out of the front door and give him a wave. In this way, he could verify my whereabouts without the inconvenience of getting out of his car, and I was safe to drink on my passes, as long as I didn't get carried away with pushing the limits of the magic ratio.

The magic ratio worked like a charm until one day in January 1991.

By this time my dad had helped me get a truck, and I was self-employed doing pin-striping and glass tinting for car dealerships. I had a great deal of freedom, moving from one dealership to another throughout the workday. I used this flexibility to do whatever I pleased during the day, so oftentimes I'd be at a bar when I had to make a mandatory "accountability call" to the halfway house. I was required to call in each time I changed location during the workday, but because caller ID was not yet widely available, the halfway house staff could not absolutely verify where I was.

Occasionally when I called in, the staff member instructed me to stay put and then immediately called the establishment back to verify that I was where I said I was. When that happened I had to hang up, quickly find the person answering the phone, and make sure the halfway house personnel could verify I was where I was supposed to be. If I ever got callback verification and was not where I was supposed to be, it would be big trouble, so I only lied about my whereabouts during work hours, as the halfway house technicians only used the technique on recreational passes. During working hours it was pretty safe to sneak around as much as I wanted.

Rolling dice with the magic ratio, drop-in visits, and callback verification was risky, and as all gamblers know, if you stay in the game long enough, you are assuredly going to draw a losing hand. As I sat in a bar around lunch time on that day in January 1991, drinking beer and watching the events of the First Gulf War unfold, I made a call to the halfway house to say that I was going to another car dealership. But the only place I was going was back to my bar stool to drink my beer. During the third change of location call I made—all from the same bar—I was ordered to return immediately to the halfway house. *Immediately* meant that I had one hour to be back on grounds or face felony escape charges. One hour was not enough time for the magic ratio to work its magic and sober me up.

What I didn't know was that Mr. Accountability Guy, the gargantuan officer assigned to verify my whereabouts, had been following up on my fabricated location changes and eventually realized I was not where I said I was. He had told the halfway house staff to give me a direct order to return the next time I called in. It no longer mattered whether or not he got out of his car. He wouldn't have to. I would soon be out of mine once and for all.

Even though I knew it wouldn't make a difference, I drove slowly around town, using up every minute of that one hour to allow my body time to reduce the amount of alcohol in my system. Desperate, I parked on a side street, got out of the truck, and did a little jogging, hoping to speed up my body's alcohol-burning process.

But procrastination only postpones the inevitable. I had no choice but return to the halfway house. Getting busted again for drinking guaranteed a return trip to jail; failing to go back and check in guaranteed a return trip to jail shackled with a new felony escape charge.

I pulled into the drive of the halfway house with only a minute or two to spare. I parked my truck and walked up to the check-in window. I hoped I'd luck out and get to skip the breathalyzer test. After all, the staff didn't give the test every single time an inmate returned home. Once in a blue moon, they were too busy and didn't administer it.

I signed in and quickly turned to walk away. I took a step or two and thought, *I just dodged a major bullet here.* At that precise moment, I heard a voice from behind the window say, "Hey, Long, come on around." These were the words I was dreading. *Come on around* was an imperative to walk around the window and breathe into the machine that held the power to send me back to prison.

I spun around and headed through the door next to the check-in window. There was no point in acting defeated. Getting busted was one thing. Acting defeated and giving them the satisfaction of watching me squirm was an unnecessary humiliation.

I stood in the office, took a deep breath, and blew into the breathalyzer as if I had nothing to hide. I then watched the digital readout begin its ascent: 0.01, 0.02, then it climbed some more. It didn't really matter where the digital readout stopped. Being drunk in the halfway house was like being pregnant. You are or you aren't—period. At 0.05 I turned to the technician and said, "I'm going to park my truck. Back in a second with the keys."

I walked out of the office, parked the truck, and handed the keys to the technician on duty. As I walked back to my room, nagging thoughts of what a loser I was began scratching at my consciousness once again. I was beginning to realize there was something seriously wrong with me. I was reasonably intelligent (at least I thought so), I knew right from wrong, and I knew what was expected from me. I even thought I knew how to build a responsible life—I just couldn't seem to put all the pieces together. Everything seemed too complicated and overwhelming.

I began to feel as though it were too late for me to make something of my life. I thought that I'd veered so far off the path that there was no way I could get back on track. Everyone I knew who enjoyed a successful life had begun with a successful life. I had never known anyone who had screwed up and rebounded to make things right. I truly believed that people have either a great life or a shit-filled life; no one could have both.

Just as I was about to enter my room, I saw Mr. Accountability Guy pulling into the parking lot. He grinned like the Cheshire Cat.

I sat down on my bed to wait for the command to report to my case manager's office. Unlike my nighttime drinking infraction, I would not have to wait until the next day to face Jarle. There was also the strong possibility that the police would be showing up at my door to take me on a little cruise downtown. This was, after all, my second major failure. Jail would be perfectly appropriate in this situation.

Suddenly the door opened. When I looked up, it wasn't the police. It was Jarle Wood. I knew that I would have to face him, but it was highly unusual for him to come to my room for a case manager's meeting.

"You've got a serious problem," Jarle said.

"I know," I responded, "I'm going back to the joint."

"Well, there's a pretty good chance you're going back to jail, but that's not the problem I'm talking about. In fact, going back to prison is the least of your problems."

Here's where the DUI thing happens, I thought to myself. I didn't think the system would overlook my offense a second time.

"What problem is that?" I asked, as if I didn't know.

"Your problem is this, Mr. Long. You are the most self-destructive person I have ever known in my life," Jarle said matter-of-factly.

I collected my thoughts quickly and asked, "That's the problem I have?"

"Yes, that's the problem you have. And it's a very serious problem."

Holy shit, I thought. *Did no one notice the DUI stunt?*

"Your problem," Jarle continued, "is that anytime you get some good things going in your life, you do something to screw it all up."

I stared at him as if I knew what the hell he was talking about. "Maybe you're right," I said, wanting to sound convincing, even though I didn't understand a word of what he was saying.

"I am right, and you should think about it. You're on total grounds until we decide what to do with you. You'll have a DOC hearing soon," Jarle said as he headed for the door. "By the way, have someone come pick up your truck. You won't be needing it here anymore."

Just before Jarle pulled the door closed, he said, "One more thing, Mr. Long, the DOC doesn't know about all your problems." Then he was gone.

What did that mean? I wondered. *That the DOC didn't know about the fact that I was a moron with an apparent self-destructive streak?* As I sat and contemplated Jarle's words, a thought occurred to me: *Could he mean that he realized I had been driving under the influence, but that he wasn't going to make it part of his report?*

Two weeks later I had my DOC hearing. Despite my best efforts to screw myself, I wasn't sent back to the joint. I didn't know how much influence Jarle Wood had with the DOC hearing committee, but I felt sure that he'd gone to bat for me. I never found out what Jarle meant by his parting words, but the fact that I had been driving just prior to checking in and blowing hot for alcohol consumption never came up in the DOC deliberations.

Within a few months I had earned back most of my halfway house privileges. I was not allowed to drive, however, so I simply hid my truck a few blocks from the halfway house so that it looked as if I were walking to and from the bus stop. In this way, I got around the rules yet again.

Although I did manage to abstain from drinking after getting a pass on the second offense, the significance of Jarle's words about my self-destructive tendencies completely escaped me.

In the fall of 1991 I went before the parole board again, after having been denied parole earlier in the year due to my two drinking episodes. I had somehow managed to survive eighteen months at the halfway house, and now I had a second chance at parole. Parole hearings in Colorado are very different than those on TV and in the movies. Typically, an offender will meet with only one or two parole board members, who will make a decision after the hearing. That decision is then later communicated to the case manager, who informs the convict of the decision. Convicts universally see this as a chicken-shit maneuver by the parole board members to avoid telling convicts face to face about their decision. They leave that dirty work to the DOC case managers.

The members of the parole board asked a few questions about my night out with Elliot and my drinking episodes at the halfway house. Since I had once previously been denied release but managed to stay out of trouble for most of the year, I was granted parole. Because I was serving time for a violent offense, the decision had to go before the full parole board; nevertheless, I was confident the decision would be rubber-stamped, as the full board typically went along with the recommendation of the board members who had met with the offender.

My instincts were correct: the board deliberated and deemed that I was prepared to face the challenges and responsibilities of being a productive, law-abiding citizen with a family.

I left the halfway house on December 1, 1991, paroled to my girlfriend and her children. It was a beautiful sunshine-filled Sunday morning. In preparation for that morning's celebration, I had stocked up on refreshments at a liquor store the night before. No more sneaking around with the booze. It was officially party time. I had spent over four years in prison and the halfway house. I figured I deserved to get good and drunk after all the crap I had been through.

It still had not dawned on me that I was responsible for all that crap. I hadn't changed one iota. I was still a manipulative, criminal-minded punk who refused to take personal responsibility for my actions. Prison hadn't changed me—I hadn't let it. In fact, I was worse than ever. I had begun allowing my prison sentence and felony conviction to define me. I was a criminal now.

It never crossed my mind that I could change and become something different—something better. I accepted my new role, and any hope for success that I had as a youngster was extinguished. I was a convict. I was a criminal. I was a self-fulfilling prophecy—a train wreck waiting to happen.

It wouldn't take long for things to escalate completely out of control once again.

CHAPTER 6
And Then There Were Two

December 1, 1991 to January 1993

NINETEEN NINETY-TWO WAS THE WORST YEAR of my life, yet it was touched by an innocence that would, eventually, change me forever.

Once I was on parole, there were no impediments to my drinking: no accountability checks, no breathalyzers—nothing. I did have to meet once a month with my parole officer, but unless I showed up drunk (which was a distinct possibility, by the way), I had nothing to worry about.

I was allowed to drive on parole, so I began working for myself again, doing pin-striping and window tinting for car dealerships, although I was not even remotely prepared to be a business owner. I enjoyed the work, especially the flexibility of working from car dealership to car dealership. What I lacked was the discipline to work at the business consistently. I had little experience and absolutely no education or training for successful business management—or anything else, for that matter. My only real experience was in starting the New Orleans business, which I had successfully run into the ground.

Not only was I unqualified to be a business owner, I wasn't even qualified to be an employee. I was a ninth-grade high school dropout (although I now had an associate's degree) whose resume included a serious felony and a prison stint. Self-employment seemed like the only option, even if I didn't know what I was doing. I also had the responsibility of caring for a girlfriend and three children, despite being unable to take care of myself. My girlfriend and I got along fairly well. She didn't seem to care much about what I did as long as I paid the bills. And I got along well with her kids; I just wasn't prepared to be a father or husband.

For a brief time in 1992 I was determined to work hard and stay out of trouble. I didn't want to go back to prison, and I didn't want my life to be defined by a trip to the joint and a criminal record. At the same time, though, I didn't know what to do to build a successful life. I knew what *not* to do, but I didn't know what *to* do.

I was in way over my head, but I didn't have sense enough to admit it to myself or others. So I pretended. I pretended I could handle it. I pretended I knew what the hell I was doing. I pretended I was an average guy with a family. I pretended I was prepared to live a normal life. I even pretended I wasn't a convict with a serious felony record. But beneath the pretense I was scared shitless.

Nevertheless, I continued pretending. But deep down I knew I was nothing more than an alcoholic, convict, and high school dropout, with no money and no clue. As in 1990, the real me was becoming frustrated with the charade.

Just when I thought the pressure couldn't get any more intense, my girlfriend told me she was pregnant with my baby. *Holy shit*, I thought. The news petrified me. How could I have let this happen? How could I have fathered a child when I was so unprepared for life and so close to having a complete meltdown? I couldn't even afford the expense of having a child, much less the expense of raising one.

The thought of ruining my child's life was more terrifying than the thought of ruining my own.

Scared and stressed, I did what I always did: I pretended. I pretended I was excited. I pretended I had a plan for handling the situation. I lied to everyone, including myself.

As the months went by, I tried to make a living. I had been unsuccessful building wholesale accounts with car dealerships, so I got a loan from my girlfriend's parents to open a small retail shop to provide pin-striping and window tinting for individuals. But with so little experience and training, I soon ran into trouble.

Within months the business had evaporated, and the baby's due date was rapidly approaching. I felt the walls closing in around me, and I began drinking even more heavily than I had before. The thought that I would soon have a child I couldn't take care of nauseated me. My father had been no saint, but he had always worked and managed to provide for his family. I knew I was sinking. I hated who I was, yet I had no idea how to change. I began to despise myself; self-reflection made me bristle with self-hatred and contempt. I contemplated suicide. It seemed a perfect conclusion to my miserable existence.

Then, on October 2, 1992, my son, Hunter Allen Long, came into the world, oblivious to the odds against him. I stared at the little Michelin Man with big brown eyes in my arms, awed by his helplessness and innocence. He had no inkling about the tornado that swirled inside my head and the darkness that filled my heart.

As I held him I began to cry. I cried because he was beautiful, and I cried because I feared for his future with me as his father. What would become of him, this innocent baby whose father was a monster? How could a child survive without a parent who could provide for him?

After a few days, we brought my son home from the hospital. He suffered from sleep apnea, so he came home with oxygen and an alarm system that beeped every time he fell asleep and stopped breathing. While sleep apnea is a fairly routine newborn condition, it was unnerving to hear the alarm go off and know that my son wasn't breathing. I completely overreacted to the situation and insisted that Hunter sleep on my chest so I could monitor his condition.

Hunter, however, was in more danger from me turning over and crushing him than from his sleep apnea, but my overreacting allowed me to pretend that I was a good father taking care of his son. It gave me some control, as I was feeling increasingly more desperate and incompetent.

To make some money, I took a job doing illegal telemarketing with some guys out of Las Vegas. All I had to do was lie to people about a fancy prize they had won. To claim the prize, of course, the "prizewinners" had to send money. I could work out of my house, which meant I could drink all day. I figured this was one career where I should excel—lying, stealing, and drinking would be a breeze.

Yet I failed at this job, too. Even organized criminal activity requires discipline, and once I'd had my morning Jack Daniels each day, I lost interest in calling one person after another. Telemarketing is a numbers game. Dozens of calls were required to find one mark. I failed not because I felt bad about deceiving and cheating people; I failed because I was too lazy to steal.

As my illegal telemarketing career went down the tubes, I plunged into a full-scale meltdown once again. My girlfriend managed to get food stamps for diapers, baby formula, and food, but the stamps couldn't pay our rent and other bills. I was too proud to use the food stamps, so it was up to her to do the shopping, which she did in the middle of the night to minimize her own embarrassment.

Every once in a while, I scored an illegal telemarketing deal, which kept some money trickling in, but things were getting worse.

As the holidays neared, I felt even more useless. I had a romantic vision of my family having traditional holidays in Colorado in the snow and the mountains, but I didn't understand that people who enjoy such holidays make an income. I wanted the benefits of a regular life, without the work.

Then I got the news that sent me over the edge: my oldest brother and my father were coming to Colorado to celebrate Thanksgiving.

There was no way I could let my father and brother see how bad things were. My father had always worked hard to provide for his family. And my savvy, smart brother had always managed to earn an honest living as a salesman.

As the Thanksgiving reunion approached, my desperation grew. I needed money to disguise my failure. I needed a way to pretend I was someone I was not. I needed a way to perpetrate my charade.

Just days before my brother and father arrived, I came up with a scheme to get my hands on some money: I decided to plan a robbery. I had already accepted that I was a criminal, so it was just a matter of choosing which crime I wanted to commit.

My vague idea quickly developed into a plan. I got a gun from a guy I knew and started casing restaurants. I found my target, a popular 1950s-themed chain restaurant. I watched it for several days, and I noticed that the manager arrived in the very early morning hours, around 4:00 AM, and then other workers arrived within a half hour or so. I also noticed that when the other workers arrived, they walked straight in—the door remained unlocked from the time the manager first opened it. This also indicated that no alarm was set.

I purchased a scanner so I could monitor police radio communications during the robbery, giving me an advantage in the event the police were dispatched before I finished the job. I decided to hit the target early on a Monday morning; I was betting that the safe would be flush with cash from the weekend business.

So in the cold, early morning hours, just weeks after my son had been born, I waited and watched as the manager pulled in the parking lot, completely unaware of anything unusual. For him, it was just another Monday morning. He parked his car and walked in, leaving the door unlocked behind him.

The manager later reported to police that as he walked into the kitchen, he heard a swinging door slam open against the wall and was suddenly confronted by a masked man with a gun. With the gun pointed at his head, the manager was pushed through the kitchen into the office and told to empty the safe, which he quickly did. Within a few minutes, the intruder had fled with several thousand dollars.

As I sped away, I heard police being dispatched to the crime scene, but I knew I was in the clear. I would be miles away by the time the cops arrived. I hurried home and threw the money I'd scored on my bed. I counted it: there were thousands of dollars. I had done it. I had managed to pull off the heist without being seen or caught. My demented mind could only think of the wonderful Thanksgiving we would soon have.

I went through the next few days as if nothing had happened. My son's mother turned a blind eye to what I had done. She was just relieved to have money to pay bills and buy food without food stamps. And while a man sat traumatized by my actions, while the police filled out their reports, and while detectives began investigating an armed robbery, I planned for Thanksgiving with my family.

In the days following the robbery I inhabited a parallel universe. When I thought about what I had done, I felt completely detached from my actions. All I knew was that I now had money. I had no capacity to acknowledge the destruction I had caused. I rationalized my thieving by telling myself that the money came from a corporation that had insurance to cover the losses. I never considered the impact on the human being who bore the brunt of my insanity. I thought only of myself and how lucky I was to have gotten away with my crime.

Within a few weeks I had planned my next robbery. This time I would up the ante and hit two places in one night. I had hit my stride and found my niche; I had found a lucrative job that I could succeed in.

On December 14, 1992, at three o'clock in the morning, I shattered the front window of a restaurant where I had watched a lone cleaning person vacuum the dining room floor. The janitor later told police that he looked up to see a man dressed in black rushing through the shattered window. Within seconds the masked man had forced him into a manager's office and bound him with duct tape. I knew the janitor would not have access to the safe, so I had brought along a sledgehammer and a crowbar to open it.

Over the next several hours the victim lay motionless on the floor while I beat the safe into submission. I emptied the safe's contents and left through a side door. On my way out, I told the janitor that I would call 911 so that he could get some help. I raced across the parking lot through the cold night air. I jumped in the car and made a clean getaway.

Or so I thought. The dining room floor was covered in glass, and on one small shard was a speck of blood, imperceptible to the naked eye. Certainly the bloody shard went unnoticed by the masked intruder, who was unaware that he had pricked his skin on the broken window. It did not go unnoticed, however, by the alert law enforcement personnel. They now had a link to the unknown gunman.

It was only a matter of time.

A few minutes after leaving the crime scene, I fulfilled my promise to the janitor and called 911. It was very early in the morning. I figured that if I didn't call the police, no one would show up to unbind him until nine or ten in the morning. Hidden somewhere within me was a glimmer of compassion that would not allow me to leave a man stranded in that condition. But I was a paradox: it was acceptable for me to shatter his peaceful life, threatening him at gunpoint, yet I did not want to leave him helpless in that condition longer than was necessary to achieve my selfish objective.

A few hours later, I was waiting in another dark restaurant parking lot, stalking new victims. Witnesses later told cops that when an employee opened a rear door to let in a delivery person, a masked gunman burst into the restaurant, where he opened and emptied the safe. The police scanner buzzed with a call of another armed robbery only hours after the first one. Yet no one saw anything that could identify the perpetrator.

As the sun peacefully rose that chilly morning, I slept alone, with stolen money strewn about my bedroom. I was a monster disguised as a suburban dad. The monster rested peacefully, unaware that his blood was being bagged and tagged and sent on its way to an evidence locker in the Colorado Bureau of Investigation crime lab.

A few nights later, as I lay in bed with my son on my chest, a story about a series of armed robberies occurring at restaurants in early morning hours aired on the ten o'clock news. Police were hoping for a tip from someone who might have information about the identity of the perpetrator.

I watched the story, petrified that I would soon be discovered. I instinctively put down my son and got out of bed, trying to get him away from me and the misery I was destined to bring him. I looked down at him, convinced that I would be going to prison for many,

many years. I ached for this small boy who had been cursed with me. I wondered what kind of man he would become. I wondered how I had allowed myself to commit these crimes. Was getting a decent, legal job really that difficult? But I knew it was too late for that now. What was done was done. There would be no going back to a time when I was innocent.

As I mourned for my son, I left the room. I went down to the garage and retrieved the gun I had used in the robberies. I looked at it. I knew I could make the world a better place by eating just one, painless bullet. I tasted the metal in my mouth, but my arrogance wouldn't let me pull the trigger.

I put the gun down and looked around the garage at the evidence of my crimes—a sledgehammer, a crowbar, a ski mask, and a police scanner. I knew the evidence could put me away for life. I thought about the news report and calmed down a little. If they knew who I was, would they risk tipping me off?

I walked back into the house and peered out the front window. The night was empty of everything except my paranoia. I walked back into the garage, piled up the evidence, wiped it clean of fingerprints, put it in the car, and drove off. I wanted to dispose of the evidence. I scattered it across town in numerous dumpsters and trash cans. I knew the items would look suspicious if they were found all together; but found individually, they would mean nothing.

I spent the next few weeks drinking and waiting for the police to come knocking. But the knock never came. By Christmas, I figured I was safe; the police didn't know who I was. Acting as if things were normal, I took my family to Las Vegas to spend Christmas with my brother and his family. While we were there, I married my son's mother at a chapel on the Strip. I thought that getting married would somehow guarantee my son a healthy family life. I had lost all sense of reality.

After New Year's we returned to Colorado. Within two weeks things were spinning out of control. Again.

CHAPTER 7

Happy Birthday to Me

January 18, 1993

BY THE MIDDLE OF JANUARY 1993, I was back in the crime business. After the initial panic following the airing of the news story, I calmed down and realized that I had gotten away with some serious crimes. I began to believe that robbery was my calling.

I bought another gun, and I had my new wife buy me a police scanner for my birthday. I decided my next target would be in Vail, Colorado, so I made the two-hour drive from Colorado Springs and skied for a couple of days while I planned my next crime. On my birthday, January 18, 1993, I was scoping out a target when I slowed for a stop sign on a snow-packed road just outside Vail. It was the middle of the night. As I made my way onto a frontage road off the interstate, a car suddenly appeared in my rearview mirror. It was dark. I couldn't make out what kind of car it was. Suddenly flashing blue lights lit up the snow-covered mountains.

My heart stopped. I was carrying a sledgehammer and a crowbar in the truck. I had a ski mask, duct tape, a police scanner, and a 9mm pistol in my glove box. It wouldn't take much for a cop to figure out I was more than a skier on vacation. The possession of a handgun by an ex-con was a parole violation and a felony.

My mind raced. Should I run, or should I stop and take the chance the cop wouldn't search the truck? Maybe he would give me a ticket and send me on my way.

I decided running was too risky. I had always believed that even if you could outrun one cop, you could never outrun his radio. My best bet was to stay calm and hope the cop didn't become overly curious.

I pulled over to a gradual stop. The cop approached my window and asked what I was doing out in the middle of the night. I told him I was headed back to Colorado Springs after a couple of days of skiing, and I had been pulling over to use the bathroom. He seemed suspicious of my story.

"I stopped you because you did a California stop at that stop sign back there," he said. "Let me see your driver's license, registration, and insurance."

I handed over the documents and waited as the officer returned to his patrol car to run my license and registration. I had never even heard of a goddamn California stop. This was bullshit. A few minutes later he returned.

"I see you are on parole, Mr. Long."

"Yeah," I responded.

"For aggravated armed robbery," he said.

"Yeah."

As he spoke, he shined his flashlight into the backseat of my SUV and noticed some interesting items.

He looked back at me and said, "Would you mind stepping out of the car, sir?"

Holy shit, I thought. *This is it. I am seriously fucked.*

As I exited the truck, the officer asked, "Any guns in the truck, Mr. Long?"

"No," I lied.

He instructed me to wait at the rear of my truck as he poked his head into the interior of my vehicle. Within about two seconds he stood up, holding the 9mm handgun. His tone was now a little more urgent. "I thought you said there were no weapons in the vehicle."

I responded, trying hard not to let him see my panic, "What did you expect me to say?"

By that time he was spinning me around. He slapped the cuffs on me, saying, "You are under arrest for possession of burglary tools and possession of a firearm by a felon." He put me in the back of his patrol car, and without securing a warrant or getting my consent for search, he began a full-scale search of my vehicle.

He then called a tow truck to pick up my vehicle and asked me if I was ready to go to jail. As it turned out, we were only a few blocks from the Eagle County Sheriff's Department. On the brief drive to the jail the officer asked me what I was planning to do with the gun and police scanner.

"I'm not saying shit. Get me a fucking lawyer, Barney," I barked.

That was the end of our conversation, and within a matter of minutes, I was booked on two felony counts and an automatic "parole hold." I wasn't going anywhere for a long, long time. All the smart-ass comments in the world weren't going to change that.

As I sat in the Eagle County jail, I began to wonder if the cops would make the connection between the items in my truck and the robberies I had committed in Colorado Springs. I had disposed of the items I'd used in those crimes, but I didn't think it would be too difficult to put the pieces together.

It wasn't. A day or two later I got a visit from two Colorado Springs detectives. They told me that they were investigating some robberies that had occurred in Colorado Springs and thought that

I might have some information about the crimes, or even have been involved. The gun and the burglary tools in my possession were similar to the items used in the robberies they were investigating.

I explained that I had no information about the other robberies and was most certainly not involved. They asked if I was sure, and I assured them that I was most assuredly sure. I had nothing to do with the Colorado Springs robberies. The fact that they'd found burglary tools and a gun in my truck was merely an awkward coincidence.

I explained that my wife had just recently purchased the police scanner for my birthday. I wanted it in case I got lost while back-country skiing and needed to monitor search and rescue communications. I told the detectives that I hadn't even owned the scanner in December when the Colorado Springs robberies had occurred.

The ski mask was obviously for skiing.

The sledgehammer and crowbar were brand new and could not have been used in a December robbery. They were in my SUV for cutting and splitting wood.

And finally, the gun was collateral for some work I had done for a guy. I was simply holding it until he paid me, and it was stored in the truck because my wife didn't want it in the house with her small children.

My explanations made perfect sense. Incredibly, the detectives seemed to believe me. I couldn't be sure whether they were buying my bullshit or simply playing a game with me. But they seemed to be convinced.

Then they hit me with something I had not expected. They handed me a piece of paper with some words that seemed familiar and asked me to read the words into a phone for recording. I had no choice but to cooperate. They did, after all, have a warrant. As I read the words into the phone, it occurred to me that they were the ones I had said when I reported the December robbery to the 911 operator. The detectives were going to compare my voice to the 911 recording.

I read the words and tried to remain cool. I remembered that I had intentionally faked a weird voice the night I made the 911 call. Surely they couldn't match my real voice to a fake voice I had used weeks earlier. I hoped that with my sensible fabrications about the items in my truck and the fake voice I had used, there was no way they could pin the Colorado Springs robberies on me.

But then the detectives said they needed to get a sample of my blood. They told me that the Colorado Springs perpetrator had cut himself on a piece of glass, leaving behind a trace of blood. They had a warrant for my blood and said a nurse would soon arrive to draw a sample.

"But since you had nothing to do with the crime, there is nothing for you to worry about, is there, Mr. Long?" the detective smugly asked.

This was it. I had pushed and pushed my luck, and now it had run out.

Even though the detectives had me in their crosshairs, I remained cool. I told them they were more than welcome to take my blood because I had had nothing to do with the robbery. I figured if they had me, they had me, but there was no point in confessing. Let them do their job, and I'd just go on protesting my innocence.

As I watched my blood drain into a small vial, I felt the curtain closing on my freedom. I resigned myself to a life in prison. I thought of all the old men I had seen shuffling across the prison yard and wondered what it would be like to be one of them. I was twenty-eight years old and figured I'd be in my fifties when I got out. My son would be grown and have kids of his own. He would never know me. He'd only know that his dad was a con. I would never know him. End of story, right?

Well, not exactly. A few weeks later, I got a visit from a parole officer who told me that I was no longer a suspect in the Colorado Springs robberies. My story had checked out. The whole thing had been a strange coincidence. My voice did not appear to be the voice recorded on a 911 call made on the night of the December robbery. And there was not enough blood evidence on the broken glass to get a full-blown DNA sample to compare to mine. The blood type from the sample, I was told, was in fact the same type as mine, but that was insufficient evidence to pursue charges.

Un-fucking-believable, I thought to myself.

"But," he continued, "you are still facing some pretty serious felony charges here in Eagle County with the gun and burglary tools. Plus you'll be having a parole revocation hearing, and with the gun and all, you're probably going back."

Yeah, I thought, *but with no fucking armed robbery charges. They cannot be serious.*

After thirty days in county jail, I was summoned to court for a hearing on the evidence surrounding the gun possession charge and the burglary tools. My attorney had filed a motion arguing that the evidence had been gathered in violation of the Fourth Amendment: the arresting officer had failed to secure a warrant or get my consent to search the vehicle, thereby tainting all the evidence gathered subsequent to the constitutional violation.

The judge ruled in my favor; the evidence would be inadmissible at trial. This was stunning news. There would be no felony trial on the charges, and I accepted a plea bargain for a misdemeanor gun charge and was sentenced to thirty days time served.

Suddenly, within days of facing decades of prison time due to multiple felonies in two jurisdictions, I was standing outside the Eagle County jail, free to go home. And all I had been pegged with was a misdemeanor. I couldn't believe it. After being certain I would not see the streets for thirty years, I was now standing in the county jail parking lot in the middle of a snowstorm, waiting for a ride home.

Words could not even begin to describe what swirled inside my brain. They had me. They had me dead to rights, yet somehow I was free. I was on my way back to Colorado Springs, a free man once again.

When I got home that night, I received a phone call from my parole officer telling me to report to the parole department the following morning. I knew I was going back into custody on the parole violation, but compared to what I had been facing, the parole violation seemed trivial.

It was surprising that Eagle County had released me in the first place. They were in such a hurry to get rid of me that they ignored the hold that the parole department had placed on me. So after one night at home I knew I was on my way back to the joint. All things considered, I was fine with that.

It had been one hell of a birthday. Now all I had to do was face the parole department.

CHAPTER 8
Back to the Can

January 1993 to Fall 1993

WHEN I REPORTED TO THE PAROLE OFFICE the next morning, I was handcuffed and taken into custody. As I was led away by a parole agent, I sensed that people in the department had been talking about the robberies. The agent asked, "So you weren't involved in those robberies?"

"That's what the detectives said," I responded. Knots were growing in my stomach. I felt that this guy was toying with me, and I suspected he might be recording our conversation. "Looks to me like they jumped the gun," I shrugged, "had the wrong guy."

"Looks like you got lucky, pal."

"Funny, I don't feel lucky," I lied. I felt like I'd just won the lottery.

I was booked into jail on a parole hold, and I faced a parole revocation hearing within a few weeks. My return to prison was certain as a result of the firearm possession. I had pleaded guilty to a weapons misdemeanor, and that was more than sufficient grounds to revoke my parole.

At the hearing, my parole was indeed revoked. I would be going back to the joint for at least six to twelve months.

When I was transferred back to the Department of Corrections in Cañon City, I was held briefly in Cell House #5, now called the Central Transportation Unit (CTU). It was pretty much Grand Central Station, serving as a central facility that managed all transfers within the DOC. Returning to the place where my prison career started was a real eye-opener—I realized what a loser I was. *How could I let myself return to a life of crime after going through the system?* I had known many men who had been through the revolving door time after time, and I wondered how they could be so stupid. Yet here I was back in the system again.

Within a week or two I was transferred to Bent County Correctional Center, a new medium-security prison that had just opened on the eastern plains of Colorado. For all practical purposes, it was in Kansas. It was also dusty and barren. I had always thought of the mountains when I pictured Colorado, but the eastern plains could easily be mistaken for a Nevada desert.

Back in prison, something began gnawing at the back of my brain. I was relieved the cops had not pinned the robberies on me, but I still couldn't believe it. I wondered whether Colorado law enforcement had some strategic reason for letting me think I had gotten away with it. I began to worry and obsess about their real plan for me. Once again, fear consumed me, and I began living in a constant state of panic and paranoia.

I obsessed about the blood. In fact, all I could think about was the goddamn blood. It was early 1993, and DNA technology had not yet fully developed, but it was common knowledge that DNA could irrefutably identify the perpetrator of a crime. I didn't understand how the police could have my blood at the crime scene yet not be able to identify it as mine. I was convinced they knew I was their man but were playing mind games with me. I was convinced they were waiting for me around every corner.

I remember once jogging in the prison yard, just inside the fence near the institution's parking lot. As I jogged, I saw two men dressed in suits get out of a car. They looked like detectives. I stopped running and began to panic. I was certain they had come to arrest me on the robbery charge.

I waited for the PA system to bark my name and tell me to report to the administration building. I waited and waited, but there was nothing. It was a false alarm. They were not there for me. They probably weren't even cops; it was just my paranoid imagination. I was losing what little mind I had left, growing certain that the police were toying with me.

Over the spring, summer, and fall of 1993, I served the parole violation. During that time I became increasingly obsessed with DNA technology. I wondered how it worked. I wondered how the police could have my blood and be unable to test it. I watched every news and television show that even mentioned the initials DNA. I read with keen interest any newspaper or magazine article I could find that discussed the technology. As I studied the advancements in the technology, I wondered whether one day the improved technology would allow the police to make a positive match to me. I drove myself crazy worrying about how much blood they had and when they were coming to get me.

And then one day in the fall of 1993, just nine months after my parole had been revoked, my case manager called me into his office and told me I was again being released to the halfway house in Colorado Springs.

"Excuse me?" I asked. There was no way they were letting me out, and I knew it. *This is it*, I thought. *They want me to think I'm getting out, but as soon as I get within an inch of freedom they're going to arrest me. There is no way in the world I am really getting back to the streets.*

During the week I waited to be transferred to the halfway house, I couldn't sleep. Each night I tossed and turned. My mind flip-flopped between thinking *I am getting out. I somehow got away with this* and *These sons of bitches are playing mind games with me. They will be waiting in Colorado Springs when I step off the bus.*

I was transferred to two separate DOC facilities as they worked me back toward Colorado Springs. The night before I was to be transferred to the halfway house, I waited in Cell House #5 in Cañon City. This was the same hundred-year-old building where I had started my prison journey in 1987. As I waited in a cell my stomach churned. The anxiety made me nauseated.

I was convinced that when the DOC bus dropped me at the halfway house the next morning, the cops would be there waiting. I still couldn't figure out why the detectives had not arrested me for the Colorado Springs robberies in January, when I was in the Eagle County jail. What could the police gain by waiting, except for the satisfaction of knowing I was losing my mind?

I didn't sleep that night. The next morning the cell door slid open and I walked downstairs to the discharge area. I was handcuffed and placed on a DOC bus headed for Colorado Springs. I thought it was odd that a person being released would be handcuffed. Was I really an escape risk at that point?

Maybe they knew something I didn't. Maybe they knew I wasn't going to see the street for even one minute. They were no doubt part of the grand illusion that I was going to the halfway house. I watched the security officers who manned the bus, who stared at me from the corner of their eyes. I watched them and they watched me. They tried not to smile and reveal their smugness about the perfection of their plan.

Putting me in prison for thirty or forty years wasn't enough. The officers had to make me lose my mind as well. I was perversely impressed with their flawless execution. I held back the vomit that rose in my throat. *You motherfuckers*, I thought. *You motherfuckers!*

An hour or so later, the bus slowed to a stop in front of the halfway house. I looked out the window for the unmarked car that awaited me. I saw nothing. I walked down the long aisle that separated the rows of seats. I stepped off the bus. A security officer freed me from the cuffs. "Grab your shit," he ordered.

I grabbed my duffle bag and entered the office where twice I had sent the breathalyzer skyward. I looked around: no detectives, no police.

Can this be happening? I thought.

I walked up the stairs into the lobby. The place hadn't changed a bit.

The corrections technician gave me a room assignment and told me to go there and sit tight until a case manager called for me. I walked down the sidewalk toward my room, glancing back nervously over my shoulder. I entered a room containing six or seven bunks. There was no one else in the room. All the other residents were at work. I sat down on an empty bunk and waited.

After thirty minutes I began making up one of the beds with the bedding material I had been given. I unpacked my duffle bag and then sat back on the bed. "Unbelievable," I said to an empty room.

I hadn't eaten in a day or two, so I opened the sack lunch the technician had given me. I nibbled at a sandwich and cookie, all the while keeping my eyes on the door. Every now and then I heard footsteps, and I froze. Each time, the steps faded into the distance.

Maybe I was wrong, I thought. *Maybe the detectives don't know what the fuck they're doing. Maybe there is no plan after all. Maybe I am just the luckiest son of a bitch in the history of mankind. Maybe I am* not *going to spend the rest of my life in prison.* Then a new thought hit me: *Maybe there wasn't even any blood at the crime scene. Maybe the whole thing was a bluff to see if I would panic and confess. Those motherfuckers!*

In all my paranoid thoughts, I'd never considered the police could be bluffing. I knew cops sometimes fabricated information to get people to confess. And I knew the U.S. Supreme Court had ruled it was legal for them to lie to suspects during an investigation. But I hadn't connected that to the possibility that the cops might be bluffing.

"They didn't have jackshit," I said out loud. I couldn't believe what a fool I had been.

Just then a voice came over the PA system, "Weldon Long, report to case manager's office."

I recognized Jarle Wood's voice. *This ought to be fun*, I thought. I hadn't considered the fact that I would have to face Jarle. I felt like I was reporting to the school principal's office.

I knocked on Jarle's door and heard him say, "Come in."

Since I had last seen Jarle in December 1991, I had committed and gotten away with three armed robberies, and I had beaten a felony gun charge and possession of burglary tools. *But all he knows about is the gun misdemeanor and the parole violation*, I assured myself.

"Have a seat," Jarle said.

I moved toward a chair and sat down.

"So, Mr. Long, tell me about this gun charge."

"Well, like I told the police when it happened, I was holding it for a guy who owed me some money. I kept it in the truck because my wife didn't want it in the house." I said it like I meant it, but just having this conversation was making me nervous. I didn't like Jarle's tone.

"What about those robberies?" he asked.

GODDAMN IT, I thought, *enough about these goddamn robberies.* I tried to conceal my panic. I took a breath and calmly said, "I don't know. I was cleared of all that shit."

"You don't know anything about it?" he asked skeptically.

"Nothing," I said.

"All right," Jarle said, "just so you know, I'll be keeping you on a pretty short leash while you're here."

"I understand."

"I'll need you to go down to the police station and check in with them," he stated. "They'll take your fingerprints and make sure you don't have any outstanding warrants. Then I'll give you a pass so you can go find a job."

Are you fucking serious? my mind screamed. *Since when do we need to get fingerprints and a warrant search? Was this part of their plan to fuck me over? Was this their best play?* my paranoid mind wondered. *Let me get to the halfway house and really think I made it. Then not only will they arrest me, but they'll make me come down to the police station to do it.* My head was swimming. *Isn't this cruel and unusual punishment? Doesn't the Eighth Amendment prohibit this kind of shit? Just arrest me, goddammit!*

With a calmness that did not betray my insanity, I said to Jarle, "Not a problem. I'll go down right away."

"Good," he said, "the accountability officer will give you a ride down there."

I walked to the front office where Mr. Accountability Guy waited for me. *Hope he doesn't hold a grudge*, I thought. He didn't seem to; in fact, we had a pleasant conversation on our way to the police department as I contemplated jumping out of the car and running like hell.

I was pretty sick of the relentless game my mind was playing with me. I had grown weary of the fear that seemed to rule my every thought. I decided to walk straight into the police station and let whatever happened happen.

At the station, I gave my name and said I'd just been released from the DOC. An officer took my information and returned in a few moments to take my fingerprints. I waited at the counter, too tired to resist.

Then, a few minutes later, a uniformed officer returned and said, "Okay, you're good to go."

"Yeah, right," I mumbled as I walked out. *I am a crazy person*, I repeated to myself. *I. Am. A. Crazy. Person!*

I returned with the Accountability Officer to the halfway house. The next day I was out looking for work.

CHAPTER 9

Back on the Street Again (Reprise)

Fall 1993 to March 1995

WITHIN A FEW DAYS OF MY RETURN to the halfway house, my wife came to visit with my son, who was now a year old.

I had been in prison at Bent County Correctional Facility and Rifle Correctional Center on the parole violation for nearly a year, so I had been sober for nearly a year. I don't know whether it was because my mind hadn't been sautéing in liquor or because I had had a long year to think about my life, but I saw things a little more clearly than I had before. But this new clarity wasn't a monumental shift; it was a slight inkling, somewhere in the deep recesses of my mind, that I couldn't go on living the way I had been.

When I saw my one-year-old son, some of the nagging feelings about what I was doing with my life seemed to coalesce. I thought about how lucky I was to be here at the halfway house, working out on the streets. I wondered how I had escaped five felonies and a certain forty-year incarceration. I wondered whether the universe was trying to tell me something.

As I watched my son struggle to face the world on two feet, I wondered if I would ever face the world on *my* own two feet. So far my life had been about failure, crime, and booze. I was having many of the same feelings I'd had when Hunter was born. I worried for him. I wondered what life would hold for him without a father to raise him and give him direction. I wanted to change. I wanted to be something other than the miserable sack of shit I was.

But I didn't know where to start. I still worried about the robbery charges and whether or not I would be getting a visit from the detectives. I hadn't been able to put those nightmares behind me. Still, I wanted to believe it was over. *Maybe*, I thought, *I could start over—right here, right now*. Maybe there was still a chance that I wouldn't spend my life in prison. Maybe there was still a chance I could be a decent father to my son.

I resolved that I would never again get involved with guns or robberies or anything like that. I didn't know whether I might one day return to prison for a long, long time, but I knew that if I did, it would not be for anything I did from that day forward. If I got pinched for a robbery, it would be for the ones I had committed in 1992. I swore off guns and violence—for good, for the rest of my life.

I got a job at a telemarketing company that had no problem hiring felons or ex-cons. The whole operation seemed a little shady, but compared to the things I had been involved in, it was harmless.

I worked in a windowless basement beneath an accounting firm located in a green building built in the 1970s. All the people there thought it was cool that I had just gotten out of the joint.

The work was a lot like the telemarketing I had done before. I called people up and told them they had won an amazing prize or that they had been "handpicked" to receive cash or a new car. To receive their prize, all they had to do was buy some crap we were selling. My job was to convince our "clients" not to worry about the money they were sending in for the vitamins or the water filter. The only thing they needed to think about was the big prize.

The job was a piece of cake, and it was working out well. Telling a few white lies and shading the truth seemed about as sinful as missing church. In my warped mind, nobody was getting hurt. Nobody was pulling guns. My boss was rarely around, and when he was, he was drunk and high on cocaine. I was making a lot of money, and the halfway house seemed to be okay with my working there. The whole telemarketing industry seemed right up my alley. It appeared legitimate enough, and there were a lot of large telemarketing companies. Yeah, telemarketing could be a little shady, but the companies operated out in the open, and no one was going to jail—at least not yet.

And I was good at it. Before long, I was managing two shifts. I had a knack for managing other people. I had an ability to read individuals, and I could usually find out what motivated them. I could make people laugh and teach them how to lie like an expert. The job took some rationalization, but I came to think of our targets as customers. It was a business just shady enough to employ someone like me and just legal enough to keep my ass out of jail. It was a match made in heaven.

My son continued to live with his mother in Glenwood Springs, Colorado, a few hours away, but with the money I was making, I was able to rent a small apartment, and they came to visit on the weekends. Things were going smoothly. I was pleased to be making an "honest" living.

About six months into the job, the owner stiffed me a few hundred bucks on a paycheck, so I quit and quickly found work with a similarly shady outfit as general manager. I also had the opportunity to get an equity stake in the business if things worked out. I was beginning to feel like a real professional. I even purchased some new suits and went to work each day wearing a jacket and tie.

In my mind I had made it. I had arrived. I had a real job making good money. There seemed to be hope for me after all.

But there was a big problem: what we were doing was illegal—maybe not as illegal as committing robbery, but illegal nonetheless. No matter how I tried to rationalize the telemarketing, the bottom line was that we were hustling people to send in money by making them believe they had won a huge prize. Sending them a piece-of-shit watch or a water filter didn't make the scam legal. One day at closing time, just a few weeks into the new job, the company was served papers by the Colorado Attorney General's Office. The instructions were clear and concise: Cease and desist.

I wondered how long it would take before the authorities figured out that I was a convicted felon living in a halfway house. I soon got my answer: not very long. I was placed on total grounds restriction until such time as my case manager, one Mr. Jarle Wood, could have a little chat with me. I waited a few hours in my room until the dreaded call came over the PA system: "Weldon Long, report to case manager's office."

Damn it!

I knocked and entered Jarle's office.

"What's up?" Jarle inquired.

"What's up with what?" I said, scrambling for a good story.

"What's up with your job and the company you are, uh, you were working for?"

"Oh, that," I stalled. "Well, apparently they weren't crossing all their t's or dotting all their i's."

"Apparently not," he shot back.

"Hey, I just worked there. I didn't know everything that was going on," I lied expertly.

"Yeah, well, time will tell, won't it, Mr. Long?"

"I guess it will," I mumbled.

Jarle continued, "Well, I'm going to wait and see what the attorney general comes up with before I take any action. In the meantime, I suggest you find new work, which by the way, will be in a non-telemarketing industry. Just to be safe, you know."

"Not a problem. I'll start looking right away."

"Yes, you will, Mr. Long. Yes, you will." Jarle gave me a look that said he knew something was up, but he would wait until he had evidence before accusing me.

I walked out of Jarle's office. I was back at square one. I would have to find a new job, but where? How? Even if I could find a job, how could I make a decent income with no experience? I considered my options and decided they were very limited.

The next morning I hatched a plan, a new scheme.

I got in touch with some guys I knew in the telemarketing industry in Las Vegas. I offered to work for them and set up a boiler room in Colorado Springs. I could recruit some of the telemarketers who had worked for me, set up a small operation, and continue making money.

It seemed like a perfect scheme. However, there was one small problem: there was no way Jarle would let me work in telemarketing, much less for a shady group out of Vegas.

For every problem there is a solution, and it didn't take me long to figure one out. I approached a guy who owned a legitimate small business that sold and installed stereo and alarm systems in Colorado Springs. I worked out a deal with him whereby I would "work" for him, as far as the halfway house was concerned. Then I rented a small office space in a row of offices just behind the stereo shop. I set up desks and phones and began my new operation. Before long, I was raking in the cash. Each morning I went to "work" at the stereo shop, slipped out the back door, and went to work in the boiler room.

My only concern was that Mr. Accountability Guy would stop by the stereo shop to check up on me. With my history, I had to assume I was high on his priority list.

I came up with a way to beat the system using some basic technology. I purchased a car alarm system with a notification beeper and a remote control device. I had the remote installed in a supply room behind the front counter of the stereo shop, and I carried the beeper in my pocket. When Mr. Accountability Guy stopped by, someone in the stereo shop would step into the supply room and hit the remote button. Instantaneously, the beeper would go off in my pocket. When I got that signal, I would quickly exit my office, slide into the stereo shop's garage through a side door, and walk straight into the showroom, where I would greet Mr. Accountability Guy with a smile and a "How do you do, sir?" Over the next six months, I used my "Accountability Verification Notification Program" three or four times, and each time it worked to perfection.

By the end of 1994, things were in full swing at the boiler room. I was making big money, and the halfway house personnel were oblivious to my shenanigans. I needed to continue the masquerade for only a few months more, for in March 1995, I was scheduled to "statutorily discharge" my original 1987 sentence. This meant that I would leave the halfway house, and that my entire sentence was considered served and terminated. For the first time in eight years, I would have no prison, no halfway house, no parole, and no supervision of any kind. Miraculously, no criminal charges against me ever came from the attorney general's investigation into the company where the cease and desist order was served. But I was getting antsy. While my telemarketing scheme was working according to plan, the sneaking around was stressful. I never knew when the deal would fall apart. March could not arrive quickly enough.

Just as I rounded the final corner and had the finish line in view, disaster struck. The FBI had raided the main office of the Las Vegas operation. FBI were the most feared letters in the criminal telemarketing world—or in any criminal world, for that matter.

The FBI raid at the Vegas headquarters signaled that it was only a matter of time before the Colorado Springs operation would be investigated and traced to me.

Fortunately I didn't need much time, since I was within a month or so of leaving the halfway house and discharging my original sentence. All I needed was for the investigation to take five or six weeks to reach Colorado Springs. That didn't seem too much to hope for. There were a lot of people in Las Vegas to check into; it could easily take a month to get to Colorado.

It almost did.

Just when I thought I was going to make it, I was summoned to Jarle Wood's office.

Damn it!

Jarle looked unsurprised. "I got a call from the FBI office, and they want to talk to you."

My heart sank.

"For what?" I asked.

"I don't have all the details," he continued, "They just called and said they want to talk to you. Any idea what it's about?"

I couldn't tell if he was bluffing or if the FBI really hadn't told him anything.

"The only thing I can think of is that they might want to know what I know about some guys in Vegas. I've heard that the FBI has been shutting down some of their operations. Maybe they think I know something." That almost qualified as the truth.

"Well, here's the name of the person you need to call to set something up. Let me know what happens."

"I'll let you know," I said and walked out of Jarle's office. I wanted to vomit right then and there.

Here we fucking go again, I told myself. *Here we fucking go again.*

CHAPTER 10
Viva Las Vegas
March 1995 to March 1996

WITHIN A FEW DAYS OF MY MEETING in Jarle's office, I was answering questions from an FBI special agent. If I hadn't been instructed to do so by Jarle, I would not have agreed to the interview.

As I sat in the FBI office, my mind and my guts were spinning, but the other details of that conversation are now a blur. I can only remember trying to be as vague as possible and desperately wanting to get out of there. The meeting ended, and I reported back to Jarle that they had asked some general questions about some guys I knew.

In reality they had asked questions about the entire organization, including the Vegas operation and our little boiler room behind the stereo shop. But the Feds were in the very early stages of their investigation and weren't anywhere near getting indictments and making arrests. I didn't know what the FBI would tell Jarle, but they thanked me for my time and said they would be in touch.

Apparently the Feds never said anything to Jarle, and it would be a year before they finally made any arrests in the case.

Another bullet dodged.

Within a couple of weeks I received my official discharge papers and was free to go. I knew the clock was ticking on the FBI investigation, but I felt less suffocated once I was out of the halfway house. I calculated that whatever the FBI discovered about me, I would only receive a telemarketing charge. I figured that I couldn't get sentenced for more than six months to a year on a case like that.

I left the halfway house and moved in with my son (now two and a half), his mother, and her other children. They were still living across the state in Glenwood Springs, Colorado, and I was happy to leave Colorado Springs.

What I didn't realize then was that the FBI doesn't work fast. While local law enforcement tend to arrest first then investigate, the FBI does a slow, methodical investigation before making an arrest. By the time the FBI picks you up, there is no point in lying. They already know everything.

In Glenwood Springs, now free of state supervision, I began managing telemarketing operations for a new outfit out of Vegas. I was now also free to travel to Las Vegas, which opened the door for me to freely engage in two exciting vices: gambling and cocaine.

Thus, during 1995, my life spun completely out of control. I interspersed criminal telemarketing operations with wild drinking binges, trips to Las Vegas casinos, and cocaine frenzies. I was losing so much money in the casinos that I was a preferred customer. The casinos loved to see me coming.

The Vegas casinos offered me free luxury rooms, free food, and free shows—anything I wanted. Being a frequent visitor to Vegas was the ultimate fantasy for me. The casinos pretended that I mattered, and I pretended that I wasn't a pathetic loser. It was a perfect arrangement.

One night in Vegas, I made my way to a high-roller room in a popular Strip casino. I had been there many times, and the casino host knew me by name. I was already high when I arrived, and I continued to get hammered as I played blackjack for many hours.

I got so wasted that I began nodding off. I could barely lift up my head to see the dealer. I just kept my gaze fixed on my cards and used hand signals to move the game along. Every now and then I picked up my head high enough to see who was dealing.

I finally ran out of money. The game was over: no money, no game. I knew I had started the night with $15,000 in my pocket, and I had another $15,000 stashed in my room. I staggered to the elevator and groped my way back to my room to get more money. I smelled a comeback at the blackjack tables.

But there was no money in my hiding spot. Had someone taken it? How could anyone know where I stashed it? Then I noticed the time: it was nearly 5:00 AM. I had been thinking it was around midnight. Somewhere I had lost an entire night. Where had the hours gone?

I began to think really hard—sparks of recollection flashed through my brain. I remembered that I had been to the room earlier that morning. No one had stolen my money; I had taken it myself. I had brought it to the blackjack table. I hadn't lost $15,000 that night; I had lost $30,000.

I sat on the bed, amazed at my own stupidity and insanity. I reached over and picked up the phone to call my wife. I figured I'd let her know the good news so that by the time I got home some of her anger might be dissipated.

"Hey, it's me," I slurred into the phone. "Just thought I'd let you know I lost thirty grand tonight, but I'm not up to the argument we're are going to have. We'll talk when I get home." I quickly hung up the phone.

Within a minute or two the phone rang, and I just stared at it. *Didn't I just say I wasn't up for an argument?* I thought. I let the phone ring. A few minutes later it began to ring again. I ignored it and it eventually stopped.

But a few minutes later there was a loud knock at the door. "WHAT?" I yelled at the door.

"Mr. Long, this is hotel security. Are you okay?"

"I'm fucking perfect!"

"Could we see you for a moment? Your wife called and she's worried about you."

"You have got to be kidding me," I said to an empty hotel room.

I opened the door and was greeted by two security guards. "Your wife called and just wanted us to check on you. She said you had a rough night," one of them said.

"Yeah, that's a bit of an understatement, but I'm fine as you can see." I quickly closed the door.

For a brief moment I saw through my alcoholic haze and realized the pathetic reality of my situation. I wanted away from the hotel. I wanted out of Las Vegas.

I left my room and walked through the casino and out into the street. I had just dropped $30,000, and now I didn't even have cab fare. I knew that the casino would set me up with a cab or a limo, but now that I had seen everything for what it was, I didn't want anything more from them. I hated myself, I hated these buildings, and I hated this town. I had to get out.

I began to walk to the airport. My self-loathing intensified with every step. As I turned left off the Strip toward McCarran International Airport, I watched the cars coming toward me. I realized I could step off the curb and end it all. One large stride, that's all it would take.

But who was I kidding? I was too full of shit to hurt myself. I was too arrogant, too selfish, and too full of fear. I continued my walk to the airport and managed to get myself back to Colorado.

On the flight home I thought, as I had many times, how great it would be if the plane would nose dive from thirty thousand feet. Maybe I didn't have the nerve to kill myself, but if the plane went down it would be out of my hands. My wife and son would be far better off without me, and a plane crash would likely mean a fat settlement for them.

Everybody wins.

I thought about Hunter and the fact that I barely knew him. My time with him was diminished by alcohol and drugs. I winced at the life I was creating for him and wondered if I would ever change.

My moment of clarity did not last very long.

Soon I was back in the telemarketing business. For one of my operations, I opened a mail drop with a fake name and fake ID in Kansas City. After my confederates had conned people out of about $35,000, I traveled to Kansas City to pick up the cash and cashier's checks from the mail drop.

On the morning of the pickup, I parked across the street and studied the storefront. I wanted to be sure I wasn't walking into a den of cops when I picked up the money. I observed employees opening up the business. Everything appeared normal. There were no cops in sight, just some civilians doing their job.

I slowly drove across the street to park and walked toward the store. Anxiety twisted my stomach. I seriously thought about abandoning the pickup, but the thirty grand waiting just beyond the glass doors was more than I could resist. Still, something didn't feel right.

I walked into the store. All was clear. I approached the drop box, opened it, and withdrew a slip notifying me of oversize packages. No problem. I walked to the counter and handed the slip to the person standing there. He looked down at it and said to hold on while he retrieved my mail. Still no problem.

Suddenly a man with a badge appeared from around the corner. This was a problem.

The man identified himself as a U.S. Postal Inspector, and he asked me whether I was the person to whom the box was registered. I knew I was in serious shit, but I also knew that lying about my identity would be another felony for criminal impersonation.

I told him the name on the ID and the mailbox was not my real name, but I declined to tell him who I really was. It wasn't a crime to give no information; it was only a crime to give false information.

"Fair enough," he said. "Let's take a ride."

He handcuffed me, placed me in the back of an unmarked car, and took me downtown.

I sat down in a small office and decided to give them some basic information about who I was. There was no point in forcing them to run my fingerprints to find out my identity. However, I refused to give them a statement about what I was doing at the mail drop or any other detail of my criminal actions.

I overheard the postal-service agent talking on the phone in the next office. He didn't seem to be getting the information he wanted from whomever he was talking to, and his frustration was unmistakable.

He entered the room where I was seated, looked at me, and said, "Must be your lucky day."

These fucking cops and all their "You're lucky" bullshit, I thought to myself.

"How's that?" I asked politely.

"Apparently we won't be prosecuting your case because it's under $50,000. I'll be turning you over to state authorities who will take it from here."

This was good news indeed. Even a common street criminal like me knew you didn't want to mess with the Feds. I was booked into the Wyandotte County jail on attempted theft charges, and I quickly bonded out. I got my ass back to Colorado, and within a few months, my lawyer had negotiated a plea bargain for probation.

Another bullet dodged.

But the fact that the Feds had not prosecuted the Kansas City crime in no way meant that their counterparts in Colorado and Nevada were done with me. In fact, they hadn't even gotten started.

In the fall of 1995, as I sat in my home office sipping Jack Daniel's, I saw movement out the front window. Before I could stand up to get a better look, a man came through the garage door.

"Internal Revenue Service Criminal Investigation Division!" someone shouted. "We have a warrant."

"What the fuck is this?" I mumbled as an IRS agent entered the hallway.

"Mr. Long, we have a search warrant," the agent restated. He escorted me to the living room and told me to have a seat.

Within seconds, the house was crawling with federal agents. While some agents systematically searched every room of the house, others set up laptops on the dining room table to document the items seized under the warrant. The Feds were brutally efficient.

As they began to ask me questions and communicate with other agents, I realized that they had already detained my wife and were questioning her. The agents had approached her at work at about the same time they began surrounding the house.

This was serious shit.

As I sat in my living room watching the Feds poke through every corner of my house, I automatically assumed I was going to jail. I was surprised and relieved, however, when the agents finished their search and left. However, I knew the clock was still ticking. From that moment forward I was living on borrowed time.

I spent the next several months drinking and peering out the window. There was nowhere to run and nowhere to hide. This was the federal government, the United States of America federal government. You don't hide from the most powerful government on earth. You just wait.

I called my older sister, who was an attorney in Washington State. She made a few phone calls and found out what she could, which was very little. She also made several phone calls in an effort to retrieve some of the items seized under the warrant. Nothing worked.

So I continued to wait and drink and drink and wait. Sometimes I just drank, but I never just waited.

In February 1996, several months after the Feds raided the house, I received the news that my father had had a heart attack. I tried to make arrangements to fly to New Orleans, but I had no money. I couldn't even afford the gas to make the two-day drive.

My wife's grandmother agreed to buy me a plane ticket to join my siblings in Louisiana, so my sister, who had just moved to Colorado, and I flew to New Orleans. By the time I arrived, my father was in the intensive care unit. Following the heart attack, he had suffered respiratory complications requiring him to be placed in an induced coma. He was breathing with the aid of a respirator. I didn't understand all the medical lingo, but it was clear that my father was fighting for his life.

I stayed in New Orleans for two weeks while my father's condition worsened. I felt safer in New Orleans and dreaded returning to Colorado. I tried to compose myself so the others wouldn't see me break under the weight of personal tragedy and impending federal charges. After agreeing with my siblings that we should prepare for the worst, I headed home, accompanied by my sister.

A few weeks after I returned to Colorado I got a call from the IRS agent who had executed the search warrant. He told me that the IRS was willing to return some of the items they had taken from my home six months earlier. He asked me to meet him the following morning at a convenience store near my house.

I held my hand over the phone and told my sister what the agent was saying. She took the phone and spoke to the agent, with whom she was familiar from previous conversations.

"Hi, this is Weldon's sister and attorney; I am acting in this capacity as his attorney. Are you planning on taking my client into custody tomorrow?" she asked.

After exchanging a few words with the agent, my sister hung up the phone.

"They are not taking you into custody," she said.

"Bullshit," I responded. "They are not calling out of the blue to return shit we've been trying to get for six months."

"Listen," she reassured me, "I'm an officer of the court and acting as your attorney, and they would have told me if they were taking you into custody tomorrow." I spent a sleepless night knowing that I was at the end of the line.

The next morning I drove to meet the IRS agent at the convenience store. I took my driver's license and a twenty-dollar bill, convinced that I would leave the meeting in the back of someone else's car.

I pulled into the nearly empty parking lot and entered the store. Two IRS agents I recognized sat at a table in a small café section. I walked over to them and asked, "What's with all the fucking melodrama?"

"Just wanted to return these, Mr. Long," the agent said, pointing to some items on the table.

I grabbed them and said, "Fine. I'll see you guys later."

As I turned to walk away, one of the agents said, "Not so fast, Mr. Long. We have an arrest warrant for you out of Las Vegas."

Suddenly, other agents appeared from nowhere. They had probably been posing as customers or clerks, but I hadn't noticed them when I walked in.

"You motherfucking liars," I said, oblivious to my hypocrisy.

"We didn't have the warrant when we talked to your sister last night. It just came over this morning."

"Bullshit."

It was at precisely that moment that another agent approached me from behind and pushed me face-first into the wall. "Watch your mouth, smart-ass," he instructed.

I was handcuffed, placed in the back of an agent's SUV, and transported to Grand Junction, Colorado, where I was held until I could be transferred to a federal detention center just outside Denver.

On the way to Grand Junction I asked one of the agents if I could use his cell phone to call my wife. He obliged and handed me the phone.

"Hey, they arrested me and they're taking me to Junction. I'll see a federal magistrate when I get there and get bonded out. I'll be home for dinner," I said with all the confidence and arrogance I could muster.

But I never made it home for dinner that night—or any other. In fact, it would be many years before I would eat anything that wasn't served in a prison chow hall.

There would be no more dodging bullets.

CHAPTER 11

The Turning Point

March 1996 to August 1996

WITHIN A FEW WEEKS OF MY ARREST at the convenience store, I sat shackled in a federal prisoner transport plane. As Con Air circled Las Vegas, I looked down at the city and thought about the nights I had flown into Las Vegas drunk and high on cocaine, with my pockets full of money. Thin Lizzy echoed in my brain—"The boys are back in town, the boys are back in town"—this time wearing belly chains and leg irons. Yet, somehow, I felt relieved and at peace. Something told me there would be no more secrets—no more pretending. I had been arrested on a federal indictment for mail fraud connected to the illegal telemarketing, but I felt the truth would soon be revealed about the robberies that I had committed years earlier.

A few days later I made my first appearance in the big leagues of the judicial system—United States District Court. State courtrooms are packed with defendants, and the prosecutors are overworked and understaffed. It's easy to get lost in the shuffle, and plea bargains are much easier to come by.

Not so in federal court. Here the ceilings were high, the walls were lined with beautiful wood, and there was only one defendant—me.

The assistant United States attorney and the judge had all the time in the world, and they weren't in a hurry to plea bargain anything. I had their undivided attention, and they certainly had mine.

When the judge opened the proceedings and called "*United States of America v. Weldon Long*," I knew I was in deeper shit than I had ever wallowed in before.

Although I had never missed a court appearance, the Feds had found several fake IDs and birth certificates in my home during the search six months earlier. Since the stakes were pretty high, they convinced the judge that I was a flight risk, and the judge ordered that I be held without bail. This provided a significant advantage for the prosecution in a criminal trial. I would be fighting this case from jail, although the word *fighting* doesn't accurately characterize my mood—I was ready to surrender to whatever my future held.

I spent the next two months in the federal detention center, contemplating my predicament. I wondered what was going to become of the federal charges and whether or not the 1992 robberies would come up again. I had a sinking feeling this was the end of the line—for everything. Something told me the gig was up.

I soon got my answer and my life changed forever in an instant. In the middle of the night on June 10, 1996, a guard's foot jolted my bunk and awakened me. "Call home," the guard said. "There's an emergency."

Right away I thought about my father. What else would justify a call in the middle of the night? He had been doing better since his heart attack, but he was still pretty sick.

I called my wife. She told me that my father had suffered some sort of setback and had gone back to the hospital, where he had died. That was it. End of story. She didn't tell me that he was in bad shape and might die. She told me that my father was dead.

My father's death affected me more deeply than I could have ever anticipated. Shortly after his death I thought back to a conversation we had had only days earlier.

"You know, son, things could be worse," my father said.

"Yeah, how's that, dad?" I asked.

"Well, I have a friend whose son recently died. His son was just about your age," he said somberly. "At least you aren't dead, son."

As I thought back over that conversation in the days and weeks following my father's death, I was overwhelmed with sadness and regret. It occurred to me that my life was so pathetic that the nicest thing my dad could say to me was "at least you aren't dead, son."

My father couldn't say I was a good father or a good son or a good anything. All he could say was that I wasn't dead, and his voice was filled with pity when he said it. I would have preferred anger, but pity was all my father had for me.

My father's words echoed in my head. They gnawed on my conscience. I knew nothing would ever change the fact that my father's last earthly memory of me was that I was in jail again; he would never know me as anything but a loser and a crook. I had always figured that one day my life would change, and I would have the opportunity to make things right with the people I had so badly disappointed, including my father. But now I was aware of my own mortality. I realized that eventually I would run out of opportunities to get my shit together.

I also realized that I had a three-year-old son who barely knew me. I realized that one day I would be gone, and at the rate I was going, Hunter might never know me as anything but a convict. I didn't want to watch my son grow up from behind prison walls. I didn't want to know him only through prison visits. I didn't want to be a person my son would pity as my father had.

Through my grief I gradually began to see my true self. I was a liar, a thief, and a manipulator. I was thirty-two years old, and I had never done an honorable thing in my life. I had never thought about others or how my actions impacted them. I cared about one person and one person only. I had never taken responsibility for my life, and my life was exactly as I had made it.

The realizations and emotions came upon me in waves.

I cried for days. The reality of my life and my father's death was more than I could bear. I began to ponder every sleazy thing I had ever done. I remembered stealing money when I was kid. I remembered making a pass at a friend's wife while she and my friend were separated. I remembered never paying a bill on time. I remembered borrowing money and never repaying it. I remembered always looking out for number one. I hated who I had become, and the regret of a wasted life crushed me.

A few days later, relief came from an unexpected source. As I lay sobbing with my head hidden under a blanket, my mind began to work. I began asking whether anyone or anything was "out there." Some people call this praying; I called it thinking. I began to think really, really hard.

Okay, I thought, *if, and this is a really big if, there is a God out there, I could really use a little help here. I know that I am absolutely the least deserving person in the world. But I can't bear this pain anymore. The pain of my father's death, the pain of abandoning my own son, and the pain of my memories are too much to handle anymore. It hurts too much, and I can't take it another second.*

I felt a wave of relief suddenly come over me. It started at my head and worked itself down my entire body. It was more than an emotional feeling; it was physical. I physically felt a gentle warmth come into my body. So intense was the feeling that it startled me. Then something miraculous happened.

For the first time in my life I wasn't afraid of anything.

I stopped crying. I felt an unbelievable sense of relief. And at that moment, I knew I was going to make it. I knew my life was going to be different from that point forward. Sure, I had years of prison time in front of me, and it would be years before I could be a father to my son, but I knew my life would never be the same.

I do not claim to fully understand what happened to me that day. I don't understand where the energy that I felt came from, but I am absolutely convinced that the source was external. I don't believe it was the product of an exhausted, frightened mind. I don't think I was hallucinating. I don't think I lost my mind; in fact, I believe I found my mind, my heart, and my spirit on that day, in that moment of despair. I am equally convinced that the same energy is available to any and all who ask to receive and are willing to accept it.

Many people have felt a similar energy and have called it many things. I call it God, the Benevolent Universal Energy that entwines us all, and I am convinced it saved my life in one brief moment of clarity.

I decided on that day I would do whatever I needed to do to become a decent human being and lead a productive life. I knew there had to be a better way to live, and I was determined to find it. I had been a cynic all my life, so it was a challenge for me to accept the possibility that there was more to life than three-dimensional realities.

I didn't know where to start, so I walked into the closet that served as the prison's library and began rummaging through the boxes of donated books. I found a book about creating miracles by Napoleon Hill. Ordinarily I would have thrown the book away the moment the author started talking about the "Law of Attraction" or "Unseen Guides" or how we could help shape our lives by thinking about certain things. I was very fortunate to be in prison with so much time on my hands. I had absolutely nothing to lose by taking the book seriously. My desperate circumstances allowed me to open my mind to concepts I would never have considered previously.

I read a quote from Ralph Waldo Emerson, "We become what we think about all day long," and one from Emmet Fox that said people can't think about one thing and then create another thing. These quotes got me thinking. I had focused my life on drinking and lying and stealing. Was it really a surprise that I had never created anything useful in my life? How could I? What were the odds that I could focus on destructive activities and somehow build something positive? Slim to none.

As I continued to read and contemplate the so-called "Law of Attraction," I wondered about the force behind it. The law of attraction stands for the idea that our thoughts attract things into our lives. It's not magic pixie dust or anything—just a simple reality that our thoughts somehow attract "things"—for better or worse. I began to think about this law of attraction as electricity or gravity—an unmistakable yet unseen reality. Was it God? Was it a pipe dream that served only to perpetuate a fantasy I needed to remain sane? Only time would tell.

The whole concept of miracles became more palpable after I read Wayne Dyer's book *Real Magic*. At first it was difficult to get past the title. My upbringing as a Jehovah's Witness had taught me that magic emanated from the devil. I was desperate to change my life, but I wasn't desperate enough to cut a deal for my soul. Besides, I couldn't have traded a box of rocks for my soul at that point.

Reading Dyer's book, however, quickly changed my perspective. The magic and miracles Dyer talks about are practical, everyday accomplishments. Miracles are simply surpassing what we previously thought was possible. For me, a miracle would be building a fulfilling life. This miracle didn't involve fog and smoke or eerie music or demonic forces. All I needed were simple, practical activities to get me out of the ditch I had dug.

Shortly after my father died I also read Stephen Covey's *The 7 Habits of Highly Effective People*. Like many of the books I picked up in the early days of my recovery, it chose me more than I chose it. As I began reading, I felt as though something significant was going to happen. For the first time I was actually thinking about my life—what it meant, if anything, and what I was doing with it. Socrates said, "The unexamined life is not worth living." It was time to make my life worth living.

When I read Covey's discussion of the "personality ethic" versus the "character ethic," a light clicked on in my head. The personality ethic described me perfectly. It defined a lifestyle that was based on pretending and getting people to believe I was something that I was not. I had always tried to conceal my true nature from those with whom I came into contact. I say "tried" because I wasn't very successful at fooling anyone.

It's easy to pretend in prison: you can be anybody you want to be. You can have big homes, big cars, big money, and big success. You can be whoever you want to be because nobody knows any better. You can fool everybody except yourself, although in some cases you can even do that. I have a friend who says, "Time will expose you or promote you." I hadn't fooled anyone, and Father Time always revealed my true nature.

The first thing I had to do to change my life was to quit pretending I was someone I was not. I had to accept that I was a common criminal, a liar, and a thief. I had never kept my word to anyone, and I had never made a commitment I couldn't find a way to break. I had wasted my entire life and had destroyed the lives of anyone who had had the misfortune of being involved with me. This was the reality of my life, and it was necessary that I accept it.

I was determined to quit faking it, even in prison. I began to disclose proudly that I was the only one in jail who was guilty and broke. Everyone else had big money and was being persecuted rather than prosecuted. Not me. I hadn't accomplished anything in my life, and I was guilty as sin. No more rationalizations, no more excuses, no more lies. I was who I was, and the sooner I admitted it, the sooner I could change it.

This radical acceptance was the key. It wasn't about beating up on myself or destroying my self-esteem and self-respect. It was about being honest with myself so I could address the problems that were destroying my life and the lives of those around me. It was about getting real. It was about keeping it real.

Albert Einstein said that to solve a problem we must elevate ourselves to a higher level of thought than the level of thought that created the problem. Until I came to terms with who and what I really was, I had no chance of creating a better life. I had to start thinking at a higher level.

Understanding and accepting that I embodied the personality ethic was much easier than instantly living the character ethic that Covey described. Developing a strong character would take a lifetime. I didn't even know where to start. Moving away from pretending was grossly different than moving toward developing a strong moral character.

More than anything, I realized that building good character meant becoming more honest. Not just "cash register" honesty, but real honesty about who I was.

Covey talked about values, and how important it is to have a strong sense of doing the right things in life. To get to what is really important in life, he suggested an exercise that I found particularly appealing. According to Covey's directions, I pretended that I was lying in the casket at my own funeral. The most important people in my life came forward to perform eulogies. What would I hope they would say about me? When I identified that, I would understand what was really important in life.

Before I thought about what my most valued friends and family would say, however, I took the exercise a step further and gave serious consideration to what they would say if I died right then. What could they honestly say about who I was?

I realized that my son could say only that I was his father. He couldn't say that I was a loving and reliable father. He couldn't say I had always been there to support him, because I had never been.

My parents and my siblings could say I had been a funny kid. Beyond that, they could say only that I had been untrustworthy and unreliable as an adult and that I had never done anything for anyone except for myself.

The few persons in the world who had any business dealings with me could say only that I was dishonest and motivated by selfishness.

The communities where I lived could say only that I was a nuisance and a drain on resources. Worse yet, I was a threat to peace and stability.

As I considered the reality of my legacy, I realized I had a long, long way to go. I would need years to climb out of the deep hole I had dug for myself. I had destroyed everything around me. I was impoverished spiritually, emotionally, and financially. My relationships bore the scars of my self-indulgence and my inability to put the needs of others before myself.

As I contemplated my life, a thought occurred to me: if I could find a way to climb out of this deep, cavernous hole, it would be proof that anybody could turn his or her life around. I set out on a mission to prove there was hope for anyone—including me. I wanted to prove there was such a thing as Redemption.

Covey also wrote about integrity, something I knew little about. He pointed out how vital it is to integrate the various components of our lives: personal, spiritual, and professional. I was not in a position in my life to tie all those components together. However, I could understand integrity as doing the same thing in my private life as I would do in my public life.

Up to that point, I had never been able to publicly disclose my private life for fear of criminal prosecution. When others learned about my private life, I usually went to jail. If I were going to behave the same in public as I did in private, there would need to be some serious changes.

I summed up what I learned as follows: values are knowing what to do, character is having the strength to do it, and integrity is doing it when nobody else is watching. These concepts became the basis of a new beginning for me. Accepting these ideas would not be easy. It would take rigorous determination and painstaking honesty to build a healthy, productive life.

Understanding who was responsible for my circumstances and quality of life was critically important to building a healthy, productive life. I had to accept that I had a choice in how I responded to the challenges I faced. It was equally important to understand that the quality of my responses would determine the quality of my life.

For the bulk of my life I had lived under a serious misconception: people who were successful in life were lucky. I remembered looking at successful people and thinking that if they had my problems, they would not be doing so well. What I came to learn was that everyone has problems in life. At some time or another, everyone has health, money, relationship, employment, or other problems. The difference between successful people and losers is not in the nature of their problems; it is in the nature of their responses to those problems.

I began to realize that many people had money problems. The difference between them and me was that they got a job, maybe even a second job, in response to this setback. In response to my money problem I had lied, cheated, and stolen. Eventually the quality of my life reflected the quality of my responses, and I was sent to jail. Suddenly it seemed so clear.

I came to understand that I had absolute control over how I responded to problems which was an exciting concept for me. We can't control everything that comes our way in life, but we have total control over how we deal with it. Success in life has nothing to do with our circumstances: it has everything to do with how we cope with our circumstances, and we are completely responsible for our responses.

Knowing that I was responsible gave me unlimited hope for the future. If I were a victim of uncontrollable, unforeseeable events, what reason did I have to believe that better things would miraculously begin coming my way? On the other hand, if I had complete control over my responses in life, and making better choices would mean a better life, I held the key to success in my peanut-size brain! *I was in control. I was responsible.* This was incredibly liberating for me.

I was not, and I had never been, a victim of the system. I was not a victim of circumstance. Hell, I didn't even have bad luck. I had simply surrendered my ability to respond capably. I had forsaken the unique human ability to make reasoned decisions. But now I could stop and thoughtfully choose how I would respond to life's challenges. The knowledge that healthier responses guaranteed a healthier life was the answer I had been missing my entire life.

I had the knowledge now, and it was time to start putting it to work.

CHAPTER 12
The Upside of Fear

September 1996 to August 1997

I HAD BEEN IN A FEDERAL DETENTION CENTER in north Las Vegas several months by this time, and it was clear that I would have to serve several more years for the telemarketing scams. Proving my innocence at trial was not really a possibility, as I was guilty as sin.

The facility where I was housed was taking its toll on me. Informally know as "North Town," it was not designed for long-term placement. Nevertheless, defendants who had been denied bail and were awaiting trial were routinely held there a year or more. Justice may be blind, but she is also slow.

I would spend a year and a half there waiting to be tried and sentenced. During that period, my time was split between two different buildings. The first was a dormitory-style building where I stayed in a square, open room with thirty or more bunk beds arranged in two rows. The small, narrow windows had been painted over. In one corner, a mind-numbing television blared from early in the morning to late at night. The noise made reading and sleeping nearly impossible, so I formed dampened sheets of toilet paper into earplugs to gain some relief.

The unit where I was living turned out to be an INS detention unit, and only a handful of English-speaking inmates where held there. But I was fine with that. I didn't have to endure the usual prison bullshit—war stories and complaints about how unfair the system was—although the constant blaring of Univision and Telemundo almost drove me insane.

The first six or eight months in Vegas were a time of major upheaval in my life. I was at a crossroads, awakening to new opportunities and ideas. Not everybody there was on the same journey, however, and between the blaring TV and the inability to watch my back in the open dorm, I wasn't getting much cooperation.

I remember playing cards with a guy who was having some personal issues at home. I don't remember exactly how the tension escalated, but I distinctly recall that he suddenly stood up and hit me so hard in the mouth I couldn't see straight.

The punch shredded the inside of my lip on my teeth. I knew instantly that I would need medical attention to repair the lip, but seeking medical attention would instigate an investigation that would only make my life more stressful than it already was. I was having a difficult time finding my serenity or my chakra or any other damn thing in this zoo, and I wasn't going to make things worse by getting a snitch jacket thrown on me.

For the next several days I had to hold my lip together between my index finger and thumb. Eventually the lip began to knit together, and it healed with time, but I bear the scar to this day. Despite the constant stress and pressure I faced in that unit, I was determined to stay the course and find a way out of the insanity I had created.

I had experienced one miracle, and I was searching for another. I felt as though I was beginning to see some light in the dark recesses of my brain. It would take time for the light to spread, but time was plentiful. I decided to try some of the things I had been reading about. If the strategies and techniques worked, my life would become better, maybe even awesome. If they failed, my future would pretty much mirror my past.

I had been in Vegas eight months when I was moved to a different housing unit, which had a good old-fashioned cellblock with two-man cells. I never would have thought a cell, especially one with painted-over windows, would be such a welcome sight. After spending eight months in the immigration unit I was grateful. No one else occupied my cell, and I would be able to enjoy blissful solitude.

For the first time, I was going to come up with a real plan for my future and change my life once and for all.

In my studies, I came across the universal principle that states, "We attract that which we fear." I remembered reading in the Bible that Job said, "For the thing which I greatly feared is come upon me, and that which I was afraid of is come unto me."

As I contemplated my life and set out to develop a plan to change it, I realized that fear had been the major reason for all my failures. For years I had feared going to prison, I had feared living in poverty, and I had feared not being a father to my son.

I was beginning to see a pattern. My fearful thoughts had become self-fulfilling prophecies. My experience supported the observations of atheists and people of faith who believe that we attract the things we fear most in our lives. I was fascinated by the contradiction and realized that I had brought all the bad things into my life. Everything I had feared in my life had come to pass.

Because of my fear I had wasted my life with crimes and booze and drugs, and I was now facing a minimum of several years in prison, I was penniless and homeless, I was a high school dropout, I was a three-time loser, and the prospects for my future looked bleak. But I decided to make my future brighter than my past. I decided to completely transform my life into something that I could be proud of. I knew it was the longest of long shots, but I had nothing to lose.

I developed a plan that I was convinced could change my life.

First, I would get focused on what I wanted my life to be like. I had a few vague ideas of what this might be, but I had never taken the time to consider what I really wanted. Second, I would make an emotional commitment to the things I wanted in my life. Third, I would take consistent action toward the things I wanted in my life. And fourth, I would take complete responsibility for working toward achieving the things I wanted in my life.

I began to implement my simple plan. Over the course of many months, alone in my jail cell, I painstakingly considered each area of my life, and how I could make it better.

I first thought about fatherhood, and I focused on what it would mean to be a good father. My father and I had never connected emotionally when I was a kid, so I had to imagine what a warm, loving relationship between father and son would be. I imagined a lot of saying "I love you, son," and lots of hugs. I imagined my son looking at me as a good example of how a man should conduct himself. I imagined that he would never see me stumbling home in a drunken stupor in the middle of the night. I imagined him being proud of his father and living in an environment that was supportive and nurturing.

Focusing on the image of being a good father was a long stretch for a man who had been completely irresponsible. My son was three years old, and I had been in prison for most of his life. On the rare occasion that I went home, I had been drunk and high.

In addition to being a good father, I wanted to become an educated man. I had dropped out of high school after the ninth grade, and I always felt like a failure because of it. Every spring, I hated hearing about proms and graduation ceremonies. Education does not guarantee success, and it is not even necessary in many cases, but for me getting an education symbolized a way out of my criminal lifestyle. I had had a taste of education while at Rifle many years before, and I wanted more.

I had never owned a home before, and knowing I would likely be in my forties and broke by the time I got out of prison, I seemed an unlikely prospect for home ownership. Nonetheless, living in Colorado and having seen so many beautiful mountain homes generated a wonderful fantasy for me. I had always imagined a log home in the mountains, where the snow would create a winter wonderland. So I imagined the unimaginable. I focused on what it would be like to have a beautiful mountain home, surrounded by lots of trees and spectacular mountain views.

I even envisioned the small mountain town where this home would be. It was a small town about twenty miles west of Colorado Springs, just north of majestic Pikes Peak. I had driven through that town several times, including once or twice shackled and belly-chained in a prison transport van. It was a quaint mountain town at an elevation of 8,500 feet, and it would make a perfect home.

At thirty-two years old, I had never been successful in a legitimate job or business. I had failed at everything I had ever tried, and I had never displayed the persistence and hard work necessary to succeed. Realizing it would be difficult to teach this old dog any new tricks, I imagined myself succeeding in a professional capacity. I pictured myself owning a business and working diligently each day to make the business work. I imagined being fiscally responsible and taking my obligations to the company and its people seriously. I imagined being a serious and successful businessman.

In addition to running a successful company, I imagined speaking to large groups of people. I couldn't imagine what I would be saying, but I had a clear image of making presentations that could possibly change lives.

Even more spectacularly, I imagined what it would be like to write a book, and I imagined writing this book on an island paradise. I recalled Wayne Dyer's reference to a newspaper article from the *Maui News*. I wondered what Maui was like. I imagined palm trees and beaches and the ocean. I imagined being in this paradise writing a book. I imagined what life could be like outside the gray confines of my prison cell and beyond the self-imposed limitations of my mind.

Although I had never made an honest, hard-earned buck in my life, I focused on making an honest living. I imagined not only surviving but also earning significant sums of money. I imagined having the income necessary to pay for my mountain home. I had never paid my bills on time, so I imagined having sufficient income to pay them promptly. I imagined establishing good credit. I imagined having enough money to travel and see things I had never seen.

I had never had a healthy relationship with a woman. In my first marriage I was completely dysfunctional, and I had destroyed any possibility of having a strong marriage, even though my wife had been a good person.

My second wife was the mother of my son. We were both dysfunctional and completely irresponsible. Nevertheless, I believed my son's mother could be the kind of wife I now wanted. I was determined to do my part by becoming a better human being.

I focused on being married to a wife I could trust and admire. I imagined a wife who was smart, practical, funny, and hardworking. I imagined having a wife who was a beautiful person as well as a beautiful woman.

There was no area in my life where I was more deficient than in my ability to be a man. A true man is a number of things, and

I was none of them. A man is dependable and honorable. A man works hard to take care of his family. A man provides a home for his family. A man carries himself with dignity and strength. A man has character and integrity.

I wanted to be considered a man of strength and character. Not only did I want others to see that in me, I wanted to see it in myself. I focused on how a man of strength, character, and integrity would conduct himself. I imagined what kind of husband and father and businessman he would be. I imagined how he would treat others: would he act fairly in all circumstances, or would he resolve issues to his own advantage?

After spending weeks focusing on who I wanted to be, I made an emotional commitment to my vision. I took a piece of lined paper and a pen. I sat down at the gray metal desk in my cell and wrote down the following sentences.

I am an awesome father to my son.

I am an educated man.

I own a beautiful mountain home.

I am a successful businessman. I am a successful writer and public speaker.

I am writing a book on the beaches of Maui.

I am wealthy beyond my wildest dreams.

I have an honest, trustworthy, and beautiful wife.

I am a man of character, honor, and integrity.

I stuck this list to my cell wall with toothpaste and repeated it to myself every day. I had nothing to lose and everything to gain.

Each day, I awoke early in the morning, before the insanity of a day in prison had a chance to knock me off my beam, and meditated on the words I had written. I began to visualize what those words would ultimately mean for me.

When I began living with a "celly," or cellmate, I got up early in order to get some alone time. The last thing a guy wants to see when he awakens in prison is his cellmate sitting motionlessly on the bunk in a trance of some sort. Sometimes, depending on the level of resistance I might receive from a particular celly, I would simply lie still and go through the meditation/visualization process as though I were simply sleeping. I was willing to make accommodations to minimize conflict, but I was not willing to use possible conflict as an excuse for giving up my focused thinking.

Meditation means different things to different people, but for me it meant simply sitting quietly and repeating the things I had posted on the wall of my cell. Depending on how I felt, I would repeat those sentences ten to fifty times as a sort of mantra or incantation. I didn't want a harsh routine; I wanted flexibility. I didn't want the substance of my goals to become subordinate to the routine itself; I wanted creativity.

After repeating the words, I visualized all the things on my list. I pictured laughing with my son or talking about things that were important to him. I visualized telling my son I loved him and hugging him before he went to bed at night. I imagined him growing into a balanced, healthy adult. I imagined him being proud of me. I imagined being proud of him and telling him so, on a regular basis.

I began to imagine what having an education would feel like. I thought about the professional opportunities that might come from learning. I thought about how an education might result in a job and income and maybe even a home. This will sound ridiculous to many, but I imagined what it would be like to wear a suit to work. I imagined how it would feel to be productive and make a contribution.

I pictured my mountain home nestled beneath snow-covered pine trees. I didn't pretend, as so many of my contemporaries did, that I already had a big home. Lying about already having a home and believing that I would one day have that home were two very different things.

I pictured myself meeting with other businesspeople and making responsible decisions. I pictured myself speaking to large groups and making a contribution to business and commerce. And I pictured myself on an island I had never seen, writing the book I had not yet begun, and being the man I had never been.

I imagined having the income to leave my mountain home for work without having the fear of losing it. I allowed myself to experience the emotion of security. I pictured my son living a stable life as a result of my income. I experienced having good credit and not having bill collectors tracking me down. I felt the absence of financial chaos. I experienced how it would feel to write a check for groceries knowing the check would not bounce.

In a matter of days after starting my plan, I began to feel differently. Initially, I felt a slight sense of hope and optimism. Within a few weeks, I began to feel that perhaps I could really make my goals happen. Within a few months, I began to feel a sense of confidence that at least some of these things would happen. I began to feel a momentum building within me, and my commitment to change strengthened.

I acted in a manner consistent with my visualizations by making and keeping a commitment to myself to write to my son on a regular basis. I wrote him countless letters, always reminding him of my love for him and that I was working hard to build an honorable, productive life. I always made it a point to tell him how proud I was to be his father.

On Hunter's fourth birthday in October 1996, I wrote:

> *Dear Son,*
>
> *Well, another birthday is upon us, the "Big 04!!" You're growing up so fast . . . I just wanted you to know how much me and Mommy love you and how proud we are of you. Nobody could ask for a more wonderful, handsome son . . .*

I didn't know how Hunter would react to me when and if I ever got out of prison, but I knew I had to keep my commitment to act in a manner consistent with who and what I wanted to be as a father.

There would be times in the coming years when I would be unsure where and with whom my son was living, but I would continue to act consistently with my visions by sending the letters to my son's great grandmother, Nana. She would always make sure that he got them.

I spent time reading and taking advantage of any educational opportunities that came my way. I couldn't waste my time watching TV and expect to become educated. Instead, I seized any opportunity to learn, whether in an academic setting or by simply reading a book.

I spent countless hours sitting quietly in my cell reading anything I could find while the rest of the cellblock was insanely loud around me. I tuned out the noise and the games and immersed myself in Emerson, Thoreau, the Bible, business books, sales books, and especially books about positive thinking. I wasn't picky, and I felt as if I had discovered an entirely new world of information. I was certain the information would change my life forever.

I participated in any class that was offered. I took classes on real estate, drug and alcohol education, life skills, mental health, parenting, and anything else that was available. In 1997, I found buried in a box in the library a thirty-day Anthony Robbins program on audiotape. The program was called Personal Power. Each day for thirty days, I went to the library and listened to Robbins' deep, reassuring voice tell me what I needed to do to change my behaviors. Robbins convinced me I could change, but I had to associate negative behaviors with negative consequences. What a concept! I studied how to run a business and how to write. I read every book I could get my hands on related to writing and public speaking. I accepted responsibility for managing my financial affairs, no matter how miniscule they were. I prepared myself to make an honest income if I ever received the opportunity to do so in the free world.

I was determined to live honestly in prison as practice for living honestly in the real world. I still wasn't sure how long I would be there, so I needed to find ways to live the life I wanted to live regardless of my environment. I resolved to repay any prison debts according to the terms agreed upon. In any prison in the United States there are convicts who run "stores." These stores provide canteen goods to other convicts who are experiencing shortages in their cash flow. The stores will provide any item available at the prison canteen, from snacks to deodorant to toothpaste, on the condition that the item will be repaid at a rate of "two for one." In other words, a jar of instant coffee could be obtained as long as the store was repaid two jars of coffee at an agreed upon time—usually within a week. Repaying prison debts was not only good practice but also doubled as health insurance. A man can get very sick if he doesn't pay his debts in prison.

I kept whatever small commitments I made to others. I conducted my prison affairs fairly and honestly. For example, as I studied the law and worked on my degree, there were many times when I performed legal research and writing for other convicts. I always made a good faith effort to perform as best as I could and deliver good value for whatever compensation I received.

That compensation could include items from the canteen or a meal prepared from items purchased in the canteen or a book of postage stamps. Regardless of what I received, I wanted the other person to receive more than their money's worth. I stayed focused on the areas of my life that needed drastic improvement and did not allow excuses to divert my attention.

I never gave up on the new life I had created in my mind. Failure and surrender were no longer options for me. When thoughts of my current reality crept into my meditations, I simply acknowledged them and let them go. Resistance would just give those thoughts power over me.

I came to believe that I was completely responsible for the process of changing myself. I could not control people and things around me, so taking responsibility meant no whining and no excuses. There was no guarantee that I would succeed in realizing my visualizations. Regardless, I had to take responsibility for the process. I stayed intent on doing everything in my power to become a decent human being. I took care of the small things and came to rely on God to take care of the big things. The outcome was in God's hands. As I began to see some of my dreams happen in my life, I came to believe all of them would happen.

I began to feel better about the person I was. I no longer referred to myself as a loser or as a thief or as a convict. I was a man on a mission. I was on a path of success and prosperity. I was at the beginning of the path to be sure, but it was the same path other successful people were on: they were just further down the line. I could live with that.

Over the next few months my confidence grew, and I began to feel healthier than I ever had before. For the first time in my life, I was gaining an inner strength and hopefulness, despite the fact that my physical reality had not changed.

In fact, the North Town facility was by far the most miserable facility I had been in. No windows, no yard, no recreation, and no library. Nothing—just sitting and waiting under dim yellow lights for the legal process to run its course. Because I was waiting for federal charges from the District of Colorado to get transferred to Las Vegas, I was housed there nearly a year and a half. That probably made it seem more austere than it would have seemed otherwise. It certainly was no paradise, but I was getting better *inside* and at that point in my life, that's all that mattered. The mind cannot discriminate between what is real and what it thinks is real. Our emotions respond according to our interpretation of events, not necessarily according to the events themselves.

I remember one day in particular walking the interior perimeter of the cellblock, as I often did for exercise. As I did these laps, suddenly I was stricken with a strong emotion of happiness. I didn't know its genesis, and it seemed unwarranted under my present circumstances—I was still in prison and would be for many years. Yet inexplicably, I felt happy and hopeful, something I had felt only a few times in my life.

There seemed to be some positive energy working its way into my consciousness. I instinctively recognized that the constant bombardment of happy, hopeful thoughts was migrating into the forefront of my mind. I was beginning to feel and believe the things I was repeating to myself. My mind was creating my reality.

This was an amazing phenomenon. It meant I could live a happy, emotional life in a parallel universe, despite the desperation of my physical reality. It meant that I didn't have to experience the negative, fearful emotions of my circumstances. It meant I could essentially ignore the fearful elements of my life and have an emotional experience that was unconnected to my surroundings. I didn't have to feel the negative emotions one would naturally associate with my circumstances.

And if I didn't feel those emotions, I didn't have to experience the misery and sadness of my life as it was at that moment. I could experience the emotions of the wonderful life I would be living years in the future.

This did not mean that I would be able to avoid all things negative. It did mean, however, that I had a choice about how I would interpret negative events, and therefore how I would experience those events emotionally. Things were far from perfect in my life. Over the next seven years, my emotional strength and my ability to choose how I experienced life would be put to the test.

As I looked back over my life I realized that fear had dominated me since I was a kid. As I looked over my plan to change my life I realized I had identified The Upside of Fear, for within my formula for success was the word FEAR: Focus, Emotional commitment, Action, and Responsibility. I set out to build my new life according to that formula.

CHAPTER 13

Reality Bites

December 1996 to July 1997

I HAD CREATED AN AMAZING FANTASY LIFE for myself by dreaming wonderful dreams. I was living in what appeared to be an alternate universe, unwilling to believe my life would not one day be incredible. But there was still the little fact of my reality, and sometimes reality rattled my confidence that my life would drastically change for the better.

Around Christmas 1996, my wife began to talk of some trouble she was having with her roommate. She had told me that her roommate was a guy she knew from high school. Shortly after they began sharing a house, however, I learned that the roommate was not a friend from high school after all. He was a guest who had been living in her grandmother's boarding house. He was also twenty years older than my wife. Trouble, indeed.

During a phone conversation, my wife complained that her roommate was suddenly becoming overly affectionate with her. She said he had started referring to her as "honey" and using other terms of endearment. He had also been telling others they were a couple.

Because my wife was married when I met her and she had developed a pattern of playing fast and loose with the truth, I was suspicious of her story. But I thought if anything was going on between my wife and her roommate, she wouldn't be complaining about it to me, would she? A few days later, my wife arranged a phone call between the three of us. I was in jail, she was at her grandmother's house, and the roommate was at the home he shared with my wife.

During the phone call I explained to the roommate that my wife had told me he was getting way too familiar, and that he was going to have to find another place to live.

"Really?" the roommate asked incredulously. "Did *your* wife also tell you I've been screwing her since you went to jail?"

No, I thought to myself, *as far as I can recall there has been no mention of intercourse between the two of you. Definitely, I would have remembered that.*

I said nothing. As I stood there in stunned silence with the phone in my hand, I wondered why my wife had arranged this call. Didn't she think this would come up? Or was this her way of letting me know?

Breaking the three-way silence, my wife (and pretty much the roommate's girlfriend at this point) began to deny, deny, deny. Having developed a little self-respect over the previous few months, I refused to dignify her denials with a response.

I hung up the phone and processed the situation. I couldn't really be surprised, could I? After all, I had been a really lousy husband, and I had abandoned my family. Furthermore, the rules of prison relationships still applied. According to Rule #2, at some point, most wives will pick up the pieces of their lives and take up with someone new. It's unreasonable and unfair to expect otherwise.

I had learned over the years that anything a person will do "with you" they would eventually do "to you." Therefore, I looked at this as my "just desserts" for having had an affair with this woman while she was married to another man. Call it karma, or call it the wreckage of my past coming back to haunt me: I had this coming, and there was no one to blame but myself.

Over the next few weeks my wife and I talked several times. One night she had little to say. I felt there was something she wasn't telling me, so I pressed her to speak her mind. As she began to unload her burden, my heart sank. I couldn't believe what I was hearing. She told me that when she had first started her affair with the roommate, she wanted to lash out at me, and she told him that I had, indeed, committed three robberies several years before.

I pictured them lying in bed together while she divulged my secrets. That information in the hands of her boyfriend, who no doubt wanted me permanently out of the picture, could be bad news for me. In fact, her pillow talk could put me away for life.

My wife convinced me that she would end her relationship with the roommate and either kick him out or take my son and find another place to live (her other children had either left home or were spending most of their time with other family members). She seemed sincere, and I wanted to trust her. I felt the situation challenged me to become a better person. I wanted to be forgiving and compassionate, but it was a struggle to turn that want into reality. I realized that I needed to take responsibility for helping to create the problem, and I tried to work things out with my wife. I battled to follow through on The Upside of Fear.

It didn't take long until my commitment to improving my life began to pay off, and one of my dreams wiggled its way into my life. In the early part of 1997, I was given the opportunity to start working on my education.

Despite my failures as a son and despite all the pain I had caused her, my mother and I remained close during my incarceration. She was unfailingly supportive and had figured out a way for me to start school while I was in prison.

Southern California University for Professional Studies, located in Santa Ana, had developed a distance learning program that I could enroll in from prison. The University mailed the course work to prison guards and allowed them to proctor the exams. This was the opportunity I had been hoping for.

There was just one small problem. The program was expensive, and neither my mother nor I could afford the tuition. Never one to give up easily, my mother talked to the school. They agreed to accept small monthly payments toward my tuition while I was locked up. I would pay any unpaid tuition after I got out, *if* I ever got out.

I was ecstatic. Now I would have the chance to get an education, which I linked so closely with future success. Furthermore, this sequence of events reinforced my belief that the things I had been dreaming about could actually happen. I had a long way to go, but I was beginning to see progress.

I began working on a bachelor's degree in law. I recalled how much I had hated school when I was young. What a waste of youth. But now I was highly motivated and determined to make up for lost opportunities. I read and studied every waking moment. When I wasn't studying for school I was reading any book I could find. The guards at North Town were very helpful and they agreed to proctor my exams to ensure I didn't cheat. Instead of monitoring me during an exam, however, a guard frisked me and placed me in an empty cell with only exam materials and pencils. This served two purposes: the guards could make sure I didn't cheat, and they did not have to waste time sitting with me while I took my exams. I often wondered how many college students got a full pat-down before an exam. But I was more optimistic than ever and grateful for the opportunity to learn.

In July 1997, after having been at North Town for nearly a year and a half, I was finally sentenced in federal court. I had pleaded guilty to mail fraud and aiding and abetting in Las Vegas, and one count of money laundering, which had been transferred from the District of Colorado. I was facing four to five years in federal prison, but I had already done a year and a half in North Town, so I was looking at only another two or three years. I felt as if I could see the light at the end of the tunnel. Two or three years in a permanent correctional institution would be nothing. I knew once I got to a permanent facility I would have access to a yard, a library, and a variety of other facilities. I would work on my plan, and the time would fly by.

A permanent facility also meant I would have regular visiting privileges. My son was now nearly five years old, and I had seen him only once during my eighteen months in North Town—for a one-hour visit through a plate-glass window.

My attorney said he could get a recommendation from the judge that I be housed in the Federal Prison Complex in Florence, Colorado. There was no guarantee, since the final decision was left to the Bureau of Prisons, but the Bureau usually accommodated the judge's recommendation whenever possible.

If I could get to Florence I would be near my son and wife, and hopefully I could get regular visits with them. My wife and I had continued to talk regularly. She was still living with the roommate, as she couldn't afford a place on her own and he wouldn't leave. She reassured me, however, that any physical relationship had ceased. I remained optimistic, and I was determined to do whatever I could to maintain my relationship with my son. As long as she and I had a relationship, I had a better chance of seeing him.

I was as excited, hopeful, and optimistic as I had ever been in my life. I had some remaining time to do, but after meditating and visualizing on a new life for over a year, I had come to believe that my life would be markedly different when I got out this time. My visions had completely infected my subconscious mind and permeated my conscious mind. My new life was all I thought about, and I already felt like a better, more productive person.

What was amazing was that the only thing that had changed was the way I thought about things. My physical circumstances had not changed at all, yet I had become a happier, healthier person. My experience had confirmed those theories about the power of the mind. I was indeed becoming "what I thought about all day long."

My positive mood did not last.

On the day before my federal sentencing, I spoke with my attorney by telephone. During the call, he asked me what I knew about any robberies that had occurred in Colorado Springs in 1992, five years earlier.

My heart stopped in its tracks. I was so close to moving ahead, yet the wreckage of my past was once again blocking my path.

"I only know that I was questioned about some stuff in Colorado a long time ago," I lied. And before I could utter another word I realized I could no longer lie about what had happened. If I was truly going to be a different person, if I was truly going to change, if I was truly going to be a man of honor and character, there could be no more hiding. There could be no more lying. I would have to face these charges head on and deal with the consequences.

My attorney explained that the investigation had been reopened based on new information received by Colorado law enforcement authorities. Furthermore, he said that at my federal sentencing the federal prosecutors would be asking for an increased sentence based on this new information.

I was devastated. The federal sentence would be dwarfed by the sentence for a robbery conviction. I was looking at forty years to forever. My son would be a grown man if and when I got out. I returned to my cell, inconsolably upset.

Had my wife's roommate gone to the authorities in an effort to eradicate me from their lives? Was his plan to put me away forever so he could pursue her? It seemed a pretty severe way to get a girl.

I never learned the exact series of events that led to this new information coming into the hands of law enforcement. I heard there had been an informant, and I suspected the roommate, but it didn't really matter. Regardless of how the government had gotten the information, the truth was that I had committed the crimes. I began to steel myself for the next day's sentencing in the United States District Court for the District of Nevada. I was going down for a long, long time, and the only one responsible was me.

As I awaited sentencing in a small cell adjacent to the courtroom the next morning, I talked with my attorney. He explained that based on the new information from the ongoing state investigation into the robberies, the federal prosecutor was going to ask the judge to sentence me to the longest term possible within my sentencing range, according to the Federal Sentencing Guidelines. The guidelines called for a sentence of fifty-one to sixty-three months for my telemarketing convictions of mail fraud and money laundering, so even if the judge ruled on the high end I was only looking at an extra year. My real problem was back in Colorado, where the state authorities anxiously awaited my return.

Eventually, the sentencing hearing commenced. The prosecutor raised the issue of the new investigation and pending state felony charges. The judge noted the information but said he would not base my federal sentence on state crimes that had not yet been charged.

My attorney raised the issue of facility recommendation and informed the court that I wanted to be housed in Colorado to be near my wife and son. The judge seemed surprised that I wanted to be anywhere near Colorado in light of the robbery investigation. What he could not have known was that I was through running. I was willing to accept whatever consequences awaited me. I just wanted to get to a place where I could see my son.

The judge sentenced me to fifty-one months—four years and three months, which was at the low end of the guideline range. He also recommended that the sentence be served in the Federal Prison Complex located in Florence, Colorado.

I was relieved that the federal case was settled, but I was nervous about what awaited me in Colorado. Nevertheless, I was eager to get there. I had spent a year and a half in a holding facility with only a handful of trips to and from court for diversion. I hadn't felt the sun more than ten times in that year and a half, and I had seen my son only once, through a plate-glass window.

I was ready to get wherever I was going and face whatever I was facing.

CHAPTER 14
Not Out of the Woods Yet

August 1997 to May 1999

I SPENT THE NEXT TWO WEEKS working my way back to Colorado. After being shipped to San Bernardino, California, I waited a day or two until Con Air transported me to a central holding center in Oklahoma City.

The facility in Oklahoma City was a model of efficiency, and it gave me a clear idea of what life in the federal prison system would be like. The facility was located at the airport, so inmates deplaned right into the detention center. Exiting the plane, I walked through a Jetway that looked like any Jetway at any airport in the country, but instead of walking into an airport, I walked directly into the reception area of the federal detention facility.

After a week or so I was transferred to FCI Florence, a medium-security facility within the Federal Prison Complex at Florence, Colorado. As part of the intake process, I was held in the segregation unit for about a week until the staff had a chance to evaluate my file. This was a routine practice to ensure inmates with enemies were not released directly to the compound. Once I was released into population, I received a housing placement and officially began my federal prison sentence.

FCI Florence is one of four federal prisons in a large prison complex, and I was now housed only a stone's throw from the state facilities in Cañon City where I had been introduced to prison ten years earlier. I had traveled a long road that ended up right where I had started.

Now that I was back in Colorado, I was able to see my son. I talked with my wife, and we made arrangements for a visit on the first weekend after I was released from segregation. I awaited the visit with apprehension and excitement. I hadn't seen my wife since I had learned of her affair, and I didn't know exactly what it would be like to see her again. I had spent a long year and a half in Las Vegas, and I couldn't wait to see my son.

As the weekend approached, I was a nervous wreck. Visits in prison are a godsend, but having waited a year and a half made me unusually anxious. When the day arrived, I awoke before sunrise. Visiting didn't start until 9:00 AM, so I had many nervous hours to wait. Each one dragged by slowly. I showered and shaved and ironed my prison wear. I nervously sipped coffee and paced back and forth across the cellblock.

It was only 6:30 AM. I had more time to kill.

I went to the chow hall and tried to eat something, although my nerves had killed my appetite. I went back to my cell for a while and paced. I walked to the TV room and pretended I was interested in whatever was on. The minutes crawled by.

I had nearly driven myself insane with anticipation when 9:00 AM finally came around. A voice came over the PA system and said, "The following inmates report for visitation." Ten names were announced. Mine was not among them.

That's okay, I said to myself, *she is probably in the next group.* About ten minutes later another group was called, but my name still wasn't among them.

As I paced through the cell house, I began to get nervous. An hour passed. Then another. As the initial wave of visitors passed, fewer and fewer inmates were called to visiting. Every now and then, however, I heard the microphone open, and I held my breath while a name was called. Nothing.

At last I went to the housing officer and asked him to contact visiting to see if, perhaps, they'd forgotten to call my name, or maybe I had somehow missed the call. He looked at me a little pathetically and reluctantly talked to visiting. Nothing.

Around 1:00 PM, I finally gave up hope. Something told me this no-show was not an accident. I knew my wife had decided not to come, but I didn't understand how, after a year and a half, she could not show up. She knew how desperately I wanted to see my son.

That night I was able to reach my wife by telephone. She said she was unable to come as a result of the weather, but she said it in such a way that neither of us believed it. Although pretending was her specialty, not even she could muster the energy to be convincing this time. She said she would try to bring my son another time, and eventually she did, but I never again made the mistake of getting too excited about a possible visit. I also knew she had been lying about having ended the affair.

I stayed busy and adjusted to life at FCI Florence, and the months began to roll by at a pretty good pace. By the spring of 1998 I was making good progress towards my degree. I had been in Florence six or eight months, and I still hadn't heard anything about the robbery charges from Colorado Springs. I began to wonder if they had enough evidence to charge me.

Maybe they've been bluffing again, I thought. *Maybe they were just trying to complicate my federal sentencing.*

I wasn't looking to have my life ruined, but I had lived under the fear of this robbery charge for far too many years. I wanted to deal with it and get it behind me. I had also realized that being held accountable for this crime was not going to end my life. I rationalized that it had been so many years since I had committed the crime that the government would be more interested in clearing the crime off the books than stringing me up for forty years to life.

Well, I was wrong. The state was a little slow to bring the charges, but they were playing hardball when they finally got around to it.

One spring day in 1998, I was called into my case manager's office and told to report to the visiting room. It was in the middle of the week, and I had a pretty good idea what the visit was all about.

A Colorado Springs detective stood up and smiled as I approached—it was the same detective who had questioned me nearly six years earlier. He introduced himself in case I had forgotten who he was. I hadn't. He invited me to sit down and join him for a little talk.

"We've got you, Mr. Long," the detective said.

"Got me for what?" I asked. I was anxious to get this behind me, but I had no intention of spilling my guts to the detective. I knew once the charges were filed and I was arraigned, I would get a lawyer. It would be up to the attorney to find a way to negotiate a plea. I wasn't going to enter a plea before I knew what I was up against. Taking responsibility was one thing—being an idiot was something entirely different.

The detective continued, "We've got you for the 1992 robberies. We've got someone willing to testify that you confessed to the crime, and we've got your DNA at the crime scene."

Hadn't I heard this somewhere before?

Years earlier, I had been told there was not enough blood at the scene to get a DNA profile. However, technology had advanced and law enforcement could now get a profile from tiny amounts of blood. According to the detective, they had mine.

My anxiety level rose. This detective didn't seem interested in just closing the book on this case as I had hoped. He seemed confident. He seemed really confident.

"I've already talked to the DA in this case, Mr. Long, and if we can get a confession, she is willing to agree to a sixteen-year consecutive sentence. This will be your one and only chance to take a deal."

Consecutive! I thought. That meant the new state sentence would not begin until after I finished the federal sentence. With "good time" I would have to serve only forty-five months or so on my fifty-one-month federal sentence, and by the spring of 1998, I had already served two years. So I still had nearly two years to serve on my federal sentence before I could even begin serving the sixteen-year state sentence. I also knew that with my record there would be no early parole—I would serve all of the sixteen years. I quickly calculated that I would get out around 2016, and my six-year-old son would be nearly twenty-five years old; I would be in my midfifties. This was getting more serious by the minute.

I looked incredulously at the detective and said, "Why would I take a plea for sixteen? That's all I would get if I went to trial and got convicted on a class three robbery felony." A class three felony carried four to sixteen years, unless it was aggravated, which could potentially double the penalty. I also knew with my record of multiple convictions, a judge would run my sentences "wild," which meant back to back to back, easily resulting in thirty or forty or fifty years if I was convicted of all three robberies. I knew sixteen would be a good deal, yet I wasn't convinced a lawyer couldn't do better. Despite thinking the sixteen wasn't nearly as bad as what I had feared for so many years, I wasn't about to act grateful.

That's when the detective revealed his secret weapon. "It's not a class three felony," he explained. "It's a class two felony." The penalty for a class two felony was up to twenty-four years and could be doubled to *forty-eight on each count* if the judge found aggravating circumstances. Given my record, the judge could easily find aggravating factors. Sixteen years was starting to look like Sunday school, and it seemed the government was doing me a favor by offering it on a class two felony.

"How is a robbery a class two felony?" I asked.

"Well," the detective said, "a robbery is a class three, but we're not bringing a robbery charge because the five year statute of limitations has expired on the robbery."

This seemed like excellent news for me, so why was the detective smiling like the cat that ate the canary?

He explained, "Although the statute of limitations has expired on the original charge, the new charge is second degree kidnapping, not robbery." I knew second degree kidnapping was a class two felony; furthermore, it had no statute of limitations.

"How is this kidnapping?" I asked.

"During the course of the robbery a person was moved into the office where the safe was located," he said. "Under Colorado law, moving a person in the course of a crime constitutes second degree kidnapping."

I couldn't believe what he was saying, yet something told me he wasn't bluffing. I had thought the passage of time would put me in a better position in this case, but the intervening years made no difference.

I began to panic inside, but I knew I had to keep my cool. Mustering up some false bravado I said, "Listen, detective, I hate to disappoint you, but I am not copping to anything. I need to talk to a lawyer about this."

The detective assured me that I would, indeed, be talking to a lawyer about this. He collected his things and left.

I went back to my cell and tried to calm my nerves.

As I pondered the future, I began to evaluate this situation in light of my purported emotional and spiritual development. How should I respond? Would I allow fear to devour me once again? I had already decided that I would face these charges like a man when they came. Now they were here, and I would be put to the test. Was I really changed, different than I had been before?

I knew in my heart that I was a changed man. I had developed faith that things were going to work out well for me as long as I acted consistently with the life I wanted. I didn't have to live in fear any longer. Yes, the stakes were high, and the consequences severe, but I was the one who had made a mess of my life, and I was going to face up to it. I had to trust in God's plan for me and my son. I thought back to the time two years earlier when my father had died, and I had reached the limit of my ability to cope with the pain. I had received strength and peace from outside myself. I had learned over the years to trust in God—not myself or my ability to manipulate the situation.

I knew the time had come for me to be held accountable, but I also knew that I wouldn't be given more than I could handle. If I had any hope of living the life I dreamed, I had to face this situation and accept responsibility like a man. Mice and cockroaches hide; men face their problems. I had become a man, and it was high time I acted like one.

A few weeks later I was transferred from FCI Florence to Colorado Springs for arraignment on the charges I had eluded for so many years. I was formally charged with multiple counts of second degree kidnapping related to the 1992 robberies. It was a brief appearance, and within a day or two I was transferred back to Florence. I would be taken back to Colorado Springs later in the summer for trial.

During the months while I waited for trial, I continued working on my degree. I remained focused and determined to build a better life for me and for my son. I believed wholeheartedly that getting an education would help me to achieve that life.

My sister, Annette, had returned to New Orleans and was now a prosecutor. After my father's death, she had remained supportive of me, despite our disparate career paths. As I awaited trial, she and I talked occasionally, and she offered to help, although there was little she could do for me. In one conversation I learned how much trouble I was facing.

Annette had contacted someone in the Colorado Springs DA's office to see whether or not there was a chance of a better plea bargain than the sixteen years consecutive originally offered. She told me there wasn't much chance of that happening. In fact, the message she relayed to me was "They want to take you off the street once and for all."

The DA's office meant business; they were tired of dealing with me.

During the summer I received a visit from my court-appointed public defender, Tom Ramunda. I could tell right away that Tom was taking my case seriously.

Ramunda was not going to lie down without a fight. He had several legal issues with the case, including the government's attempt to circumvent the statute of limitations by charging something other than robbery. I was amazed that a public defender would drive the forty-five minutes to Florence to strategize for my defense. I developed extraordinary respect for the men and women who work in the public defender's office. Tom Ramunda was my best and only hope, and I knew I was lucky to get such a smart and aggressive attorney.

After his second visit to Florence, Ramunda told me that I would be transferred back to Colorado Springs shortly thereafter for the trial.

In the summer of 1998, after years of dodging bullets, I was transferred to Colorado Springs to face trial for the 1992 robberies. The two deputies who transported me were the talkative sort, and they seemed to derive significant pleasure from my plight. During the forty-five-minute drive back to Colorado Springs, they let me know how screwed I was and that I would be going back to state prison for many years after I had finished my federal prison term.

I spent the summer and fall of that year in the county jail preparing for trial. Tom Ramunda spent significant time working on the case, preparing numerous pretrial motions. He challenged everything the government brought forward. He argued that there were serious Fourth Amendment violations related to the original traffic stop in 1992, which had initiated the original investigation, and that the evidence of my possession of the 9mm should be suppressed.

As I pored over documents the government had supplied during the discovery process, I came across some explosive information. Buried among the papers was a report that stated the Colorado Bureau of Investigation crime lab had destroyed the blood evidence that had been collected at one of the crime scenes in 1992.

The state's destruction of the blood evidence was potentially fatal for the prosecution. The government's case was based on my DNA being at the crime scene. According to the report I found, the blood evidence had been routinely destroyed in 1995. We had already determined that the detective I had seen in Florence was bluffing about having my DNA profile at the scene. He was basing his investigation on information that I had confessed to the crimes; he had just assumed the blood would be tested later and linked to me. But if there was no blood, there could be no DNA testing.

Ramunda filed a motion to dismiss the case, arguing that the state's action of destroying the blood evidence prevented me from having it tested to prove it wasn't mine. He argued that far from proving my guilt, the blood evidence would prove my innocence. It was a risky maneuver, but Ramunda was an aggressive lawyer.

I knew this ploy was risky because I knew the blood was mine. But like any good attorney, Ramunda never asked me whether I was guilty. He just assumed I was innocent. He figured there was little or no risk since the blood had been destroyed, so why not play it to our advantage?

The whole situation was making me nervous. I was supposed to face these charges like a man, yet somehow I was assigned this excellent lawyer who was prepared to concede nothing. Everything was upside down. Convicts are supposed to raise hell about the pathetic performance of their lawyers, but I had a guy who was doing everything in his power to give me a second chance at life.

Just days before the beginning of jury selection, Ramunda argued the motion to dismiss before the trial judge. The judge had to decide whether or not I was prejudiced by the destruction of the blood evidence, and whether or not to dismiss the entire case.

As it turned out, the prosecutor in this case was pretty good, too. He wasn't about to have the case dismissed without a major fight. Where were all the overworked, understaffed lawyers who didn't give a damn? These guys were Vincent Bugliosi and Gerry Spence.

The state's attorney argued that whether or not the blood evidence had been destroyed did not make or break their case. They still had blood-typing results from 1992 that confirmed a match between my blood type and the blood type found at the scene. Sure, it wasn't as damning as a DNA match, but that would be an issue for the jury to consider. Furthermore, the government argued, they also had at least one witness who would testify that I had confessed to the crime years earlier.

Finally the prosecutor said something that made me sit straight up in my chair. The government wanted the opportunity to search the evidence lab. They believed there was a possibility that the report that stated the blood had been destroyed was wrong. Before the judge made a final decision, the government argued, they should be granted the opportunity to search for the blood.

The judge granted their request. They had twenty-four hours to see what they could come up with.

Nervous didn't even begin to describe my condition. Did the prosecutor know something we didn't? Why would they make such a request unless they had reason to believe the blood had been preserved?

I returned to the jail and waited to see what the morning would bring. I had done a lot of time over the years under a lot of extreme circumstances, but this time the anxiety was indescribable. If the prosecution found the blood, they would crucify me. After all, we had claimed the blood would exonerate me, and that somehow I was prejudiced by not having it available.

I had lived in fear for years that one day the blood would be my undoing. Now people were combing through an evidence lab looking for it. Why had I allowed Ramunda to try to exploit the absence of this blood? We should have left it well enough alone and simply proceeded to trial. Bringing a motion to dismiss the case because the blood could have proven my innocence was preposterous. I was guilty as sin, and I had no business playing this game.

The look on Ramunda's face the next morning told me they had located the blood.

The prosecution explained to the judge that they had, indeed, found both the blood from the crime scene and the sample taken from me during the original 1992 investigation. It had been sent from the Colorado Bureau of Investigation back to the Colorado Springs Police Department for long-term storage, and an evidence technician had found it. The report on which we had relied was wrong. The blood had never been destroyed.

I was finished.

The prosecutor then explained that since I had been so sure a test of the blood would prove my innocence, we should go ahead and do the DNA testing. It was the least the government could do for me. They certainly did not want to prejudice the defense by not performing the DNA tests.

The judge turned to Tom Ramunda, who had apparently considered the possibility that the blood would be found and had formulated an alternative plan. "Your Honor," Ramunda said, "trial is set to begin in a few days, and there is no way to perform DNA testing in that short amount of time. My client, Mr. Long, is guaranteed a speedy trial under the Sixth and Fourteenth Amendments to the United States Constitution. Therefore, to have the blood tested, the defense would have to waive the right to a speedy trial, and we are not willing to do any such thing.

"Therefore," he continued, "I motion that the blood evidence be suppressed under a Brady violation." A Brady violation was a rule announced by the U.S. Supreme Court in *Brady v. Maryland* that the state's evidence could be suppressed if not properly disclosed to the defense.

In this case, Ramunda was arguing that the state had had this evidence for many years, and if they had wanted to test it, they should have tested it years earlier. They had no right to ask me to waive a speedy trial to facilitate testing at this late date.

The prosecutor argued that up until that day, they hadn't known the blood was available. They couldn't have tested it sooner because they, too, thought it had been destroyed.

The judge listened to both sides and pronounced his ruling.

The blood evidence would be suppressed. The government would not be allowed time to perform DNA testing.

I couldn't believe what I heard. Ramunda had somehow pulled a rabbit out of thin air. He had convinced the judge to suppress the government's key evidence against me. He had taken me right to the edge of utter disaster, and then he had thrown me a lifeline at the last possible moment. As the judge concluded the proceeding, Ramunda leaned over to me and said to call him when I got back to the jail. Trial would begin Monday.

I called Tom that afternoon and congratulated him on a spectacular job. I would someday have a life again because of his efforts.

I thanked him and said, "Go get me a deal, Tom."

"Are you crazy?" he asked. "There is no way they'll convict you without the blood. We're going to get an acquittal. Why would you want a plea bargain?"

"Listen, Tom, I know you want to beat these guys, but you've already won. The government will be willing to cut a deal now. If I can get a deal, even if they want a few years, my son will still be a kid when I get out. If I go to trial and lose, my son's kids won't even be kids when I get out. If I lose at trial, I'll leave the joint a very old man—maybe even in a pine box. Get me a deal!"

I had learned that there was no such thing as a sure thing in criminal court. Prosecutors could be very persuasive to a jury. This was my chance to get a deal that would ensure a second chance for me and my son. I wasn't going to get greedy and blow it. I would take whatever deal Tom could get.

Tom got the government to dismiss all but one of the criminal counts and agree to a sentence with a fourteen-year maximum in exchange for my guilty plea. Additionally, they would not oppose the sentence being served concurrently with my federal sentence. This would mean I would be serving both sentences at the same time, effectively reducing the total number of years I would have to serve.

The plea bargain guaranteed that I would have another chance to live my life as a free man.

I was sentenced a few months later, and by that time I had served nearly three years on my federal sentence and had made significant progress toward turning my life around. I remained optimistic that my future would be different than my past. I was focused and committed to making a better life for me and my son.

The resolution of the state case was the final hurdle to overcome. There would be more time to serve, but I would be out while my son was still young. At sentencing I presented my case to Chief Judge Gilbert Martinez. I explained my plan and my commitment to a productive lifestyle.

Despite my poor record of success, Judge Martinez showed me mercy. After I told him my story he said, "Mr. Long, I am going to give you a sentence that will allow you to get out of prison a relatively young man. Only time will tell if you are sincere, but I am going to give you another chance."

I was sentenced to nine years in the Colorado Department of Corrections to be served concurrently with my federal sentence. Furthermore, Judge Martinez sentenced me *nunc pro tunc*, which is Latin for "now for then," effectively giving me credit for the time I had already served on the federal charges. When all was said and done, this meant that I would serve about another five years.

I was going to get another chance at life, and I wasn't going to waste it. I was determined never to commit another crime as long as I lived. I would live by the rules, and I would live my life according to the new principles of honor and integrity I had learned about. I would continue my education, and I would continue to visualize and meditate on a better life. I would be a father to my son and give him the life he deserved.

Based on the amount of time I had left, my son would be only ten or eleven years old when I got out.

As I rode shackled and handcuffed in the back of the car that transported me back to Florence, I felt a calm I hadn't felt since that day years earlier when I had prayed so desperately for relief from the pain of my life. For all practical purposes, the insanity that had defined my life for so many years was over. O-V-E-R.

The years I had yet to serve seemed inconsequential. I would be out and have another chance to build my dream, and I was more determined than ever to stay focused and committed to that vision.

I remembered a quote from Henry David Thoreau: "If one advances confidently in the direction of his dreams and endeavors to live the life which he has imagined, he will meet with a success unexpected in common hours." I had read and repeated that quote hundreds of times over the previous two years. I had read it so many times I had come to believe it.

As the highway twisted through the canyons toward Florence, I felt sure of three things. First, things were working out according to The Upside of Fear in a miraculous fashion. Second, the remainder of my plan would eventually come to fruition. Third, a force larger than me and the obstacles around me was responsible for the outcome.

It was a beautiful day for a drive.

I contemplated the life I would one day live. I became increasingly excited as my confidence grew. My life and my son's life were going to be different. As long as I stayed focused on the visions in my mind's eye and conducted myself in a manner consistent with what I claimed I wanted, my visions would happen. There would be challenges and obstacles, but there would also be opportunities for an awesome life.

I would soon see signs of both.

CHAPTER 15
Finished with the Feds

May 14, 1999 to December 10, 1999

SHORTLY AFTER MY RETURN TO FLORENCE, I was approached by a convict from Los Angeles who had a couple of questions about his drug convictions. I had earned a reputation for being able to help guys with legal questions without ripping them off.

Of all the scams used in prisons to make a buck, the worst is giving a man false hope of beating his case and returning home to his family. It's especially cruel when so many young men are serving twenty-five, thirty, or forty years on drug cases and are desperate to find a way out.

In an effort to exploit these desperate men, many "jailhouse lawyers" will convince them that their convictions are somehow invalid and tell them that for the right amount of money it can be fixed. The stories used to convince these men are sometimes bizarre.

There are stories of "secret courts" in Washington, D.C., where men are set free from illegal convictions. Some inmates whispered that because the U.S. flag had been hung upside down in the court where they were convicted, their convictions were illegal, and with closely held secret information they could be set free. And there are stories of special "maritime courts" where criminal convictions are routinely overturned and men are set free. These maritime courts were rumored to have special constitutional powers that trump U.S. district courts. The trick was to know *how* to get one's case out of district court and into the maritime courts.

The most bizarre scam I ever heard involved a group of guys who had been convinced that, for a hefty fee, they would be whisked away on a secret midnight flight to a top secret government island, where they would build a new civilization. It was all sanctioned by the federal government, and all that was needed was to have their family members send money to a post office box.

It's hard to believe that sane men would believe these stories, much less have their families send $1,500 to a stranger, but a desperate man will believe anything. And there are always people ready to profit from false hope.

It was within the context of this environment that I was asked a simple question. As we leaned against the second tier handrail, the convict asked me to read a federal statute and part of a case. He then asked if the case could be interpreted a certain way. If his interpretation was correct, he felt that he might have finally found a way out of his nearly thirty-year sentence for dealing drugs.

I briefly read the information and gave him an answer within five minutes. I explained that the statute probably didn't mean what he thought it meant, but I was as tactful as I could be. I was all too aware of "kill the messenger" syndrome. He thanked me for my time and that was it.

At least I thought that was it.

A few days later I walked into my cell, sat down on my bunk, and began taking off my shoes. I looked up just in time to see a man rushing toward me, swinging his fist wildly, and screaming something about screwing around in his business.

I tried to get up, but I had no time. He lunged at me. I saw someone else step in front of the small window in the cell door, watching for the guards. This meant serious business. We were going to have to work this out between ourselves.

The maniac swinging his arms lunged on top of me, pushing us both back onto my bunk. He didn't have room to hit me, so I wrapped my arms around him in a bear hug. He thrashed around in my arms, but I was not going to loosen my grip on him until I could roll over and get the upper hand. After a few moments, he gave up struggling and became still, although he still continued to mumble about me getting in his business.

I let him loose and pushed back. Now we were both standing up in the cell. The fight had drained him, so I asked what was going on. Between deep breaths he explained that he was charging a guy to do some work on his case, and I had told the guy he was getting ripped off.

I immediately made the connection with the conversation I had had a few days earlier. The guy who had asked the question had said nothing about paying another inmate for the favorable interpretation, and I had most certainly never said anything about him getting ripped off. He had asked me a simple question, and I had told him a simple answer. End of story. My explanation seemed to make sense to the guy standing in my cell, and the situation quickly de-escalated.

Just when I thought this comedy jailhouse assault was coming to its well-deserved conclusion, the guy from outside the cell stepped in and asked where I had been the previous several months. "I had some old state charges," I responded, confounded by his interest. "It took a few months to work out a plea. What's it to you?"

"What it is to me," he said, "is that I want to see some paperwork on those charges. You've got forty-eight hours to show me something, or your ass is done on this yard."

I stood there in stunned silence. For several very stressful months I had been fighting for my life against these charges and the government's intention of taking me "off the street once and for all." Now these convicts were threatening me over the same damn charges. It's not uncommon in federal prison for an inmate to be pulled out to testify against someone else in the hopes of getting lenient treatment. This guy assumed that I had been cooperating with the government and had gone to testify at someone else's trial.

I knew I had to show them something. Life in prison is hard enough without having other convicts label you as a rat. If I didn't show them some evidence, it wouldn't be safe for me to walk the yard.

The next day I showed them the charges and some other legal paperwork related to the plea bargain and sentencing, and from that day forward I never had a cross word with those two men. I learned to keep my mouth shut, and I became very judicious in response to any questions about the law.

This event confirmed there would be challenges, but soon something else happened to confirm that The Upside of Fear was unfolding right on schedule.

Soon after returning to Florence, I finished my last two courses and received my bachelor's degree. This ninth-grade high school dropout was now a college graduate.

Graduation was a significant accomplishment for me, and it symbolized the progress I felt I was making in my life. I agree with those who say that education is no guarantee for success. But for me, getting an education took on an enormous significance with respect to emotional and professional development. I had always been self-conscious about my lack of education, and I felt getting an education was a critical component of building a productive life. It didn't matter to me that I had gone to the State Pen, not Penn State. I took enormous pride in receiving my degree, regardless of the circumstances under which I earned it.

During much of my time in Florence I worked as a tutor in the Education Department. The programs there offered instruction for those hoping to earn a GED, as well as training for various trades and other programs. I respected the men who sought training and new opportunities, especially those seeking their GED.

Following the completion of my degree I was asked by the school administration to deliver a short program at a commencement ceremony. The ceremony would recognize nearly one hundred men who had completed various training programs or had received a GED during the preceding year. Furthermore, the program would include a keynote by the man who had been instrumental in developing the GED program in Colorado. I was excited about the prospect of addressing this group of men as well as the prison and school administration.

I didn't think it was mere coincidence that I was offered this opportunity. As I worked on my presentation over the next few weeks, I couldn't help but think of all the times I had visualized speaking before a large group. My visualizations had always centered on a large audience in a professional or motivational setting, but this was as good a place to start as any. Although this was on a small scale, I took seriously the chance to reach others in my situation, and to confirm that The Upside of Fear continued to unfold as it was supposed to.

I chose personal responsibility as the central theme of my presentation. I believed then as I believe now that the key to turning around a less than fulfilling life is to accept complete responsibility for one's current circumstances and quality of life. Until a person accepts responsibility for where he is, he has little hope of taking responsibility for where he is going.

This was a risky subject considering my target audience. I had read that one should consider one's audience when developing a presentation, and I realized that personal responsibility might not be a good topic for a group of individuals who spent considerable time and energy blaming others for their predicaments. Nevertheless, this was a rare opportunity to say something relevant and meaningful to my fellow convicts, and I knew this was a critical, if not entirely welcome, message.

When I stood up to deliver my presentation, I gazed out over the more than one hundred people in the crowd and beamed with confidence. I had read that many people fear public speaking, but I welcomed the opportunity to inspire and help others.

I spoke to my fellow convicts that day about how we must not view ourselves as victims of circumstances, living at the mercy of the system, if we ever hoped to build lives of independence and productivity. I talked to them about taking responsibility for ruining our lives and for building new and better ones. We had choices, and the bad choices we had made explained our circumstances and the quality of our lives. If we wanted better lives, we had to make better choices. We, and we alone, were responsible for our lives.

I was dumbstruck at the reaction I got from the crowd. Following the ceremony, I was approached by many men who said that the message I gave them was the message they needed to hear. I realized that so many of these men wanted a better life, but simply didn't know where to begin. It's so easy to blame others for our quality of life, but doing so ensures more of the same. I knew that day that my presentation and my ability to reach others was a sign of things to come. I continued to know in my heart that I was benefiting from my study and my plan, and that a better future awaited my son and me.

On December 10, 1999, I finished my federal prison sentence. I had served forty-five months on my fifty-one-month term, and now that part of my sentence was behind me. I would now be transferred back to the Colorado Department of Corrections to serve the remainder of my time on the robbery conviction.

CHAPTER 16

The Prodigal Son Returns to Cañon City

December 10, 1999 to October 2002

I SAT NERVOUSLY IN THE FCI Florence receiving and discharge unit. I had just ended the most amazing three and a half years of my life. I had grown more in that time than at any other time. I had come to realize important realities of who I truly had been as a person and who I could become. It seemed a little pathetic that at thirty-five years old I was just beginning to see the light of day, but I was enormously grateful that I was clearly seeing myself and my life for the first time.

I looked back over the previous three and a half years with enormous pride in what I had accomplished. For the first time I had weathered the storms in my life with dignity and was living a more emotionally mature life. I was measuring my responses to occurrences instead of reacting without thinking. And my life was getting better as a result. I was more confident than ever that my life was meaningful.

My life didn't look any different on the outside, but inside everything had changed. On the inside, I was living as well as the freest, wealthiest man in the world. For the first time in my life I was happy—happy with who I was and where I was going.

Metaphorically, of course. I was, after all, on my way back to a familiar place.

Man's Search for Meaning, an amazing book by Viktor Frankl, helped me keep my life in perspective. Frankl was a Holocaust survivor. During his years in Nazi concentration camps, he wondered why some experienced their suffering so deeply while others managed to remain more stoic. The miserable experience each suffered was the same, yet each dealt with it differently. Why?

Frankl concluded that the individual's experience depended on how the individual perceived his or her suffering. Those who attached significance to the experience seemed to cope better than those who viewed their suffering as meaningless.

The book moved me in two ways. First, I realized that the conditions I experienced were a joke compared to conditions in the concentration camps. Second, I was determined to find some meaning in all the suffering I had visited on myself and others. I would ensure that the suffering served a purpose.

I came to believe that my experiences could benefit me and others like me. I decided that my problems would be grist for the mill of my life. I would use my experiences as motivation for building a better life and to help others overcome challenges in their lives. Whether suffering is self-inflicted or not, it is still suffering. I began to think I could help others overcome their suffering and build happier lives.

A lot had changed in the twelve years since I had first arrived at the Colorado Department of Corrections. A new diagnostic and reception facility had been built in Denver, although I still thought calling it "reception" was a bit of a stretch.

It was a little depressing when I was reissued the same number I'd had years before—57676. I thought back to the fear and uncertainty of my first trip through the system. I thought back to the difficult years that followed my incarceration in 1987 and how foolish I had been. I was no longer a "fish" in the system. In fact, I was kind of an old-timer.

I had a new perspective, and I knew that my old life was behind me. I was pleased that I could see my life from a higher elevation, and I was pleased that the years I was serving this time around would be my last. I would never be locked up again. I liked the way that sounded. I loved the way it felt.

I had lived so many years out of control that I seemed at times to be unable to influence the quality of my life. Now I understood that while I had no control over things outside myself, I had total control over how I reacted to those things. Knowing that it was my reaction to challenges that determined the quality of my life gave me a tremendous amount of hope. There is nothing more debilitating than being powerless, and there is nothing more pathetic than acting powerless when we are not.

The power to decide is ours and ours alone. Only a fool surrenders it.

I had about four years remaining on my state sentence, but with "good time" factored in, I was facing a max of about three and a half years. I would also have several chances for parole in the years ahead.

After Y2K came and went without the computers malfunctioning and releasing the entire prison population, I was transferred to Four Mile Correctional Center in beautiful Cañon City, Colorado. Four Mile was a medium/low-security facility that housed a dairy farm as part of the prison industries program. Many of the inmates worked in the dairy, milking cows or driving tractors or whatever the hell people do on a dairy farm. There were plenty of fences and plenty of cops at Four Mile, but the cows made it seem less like prison.

Most of the guys at Four Mile were relatively "short." This was no reflection on their physical stature; it meant that they had five years or less to serve, a radical departure from FCI Florence, where most of the inmates had many, many years ahead of them, and some would never get out at all. It's a different attitude and a different environment when guys aren't walking around with forty years to serve. It was a lot less stressful, and I was happy to be there.

Still, all the same games went on in Four Mile, just on a smaller scale, since most of the guys thought more about going home than how they were going to live their lives in prison.

I had served four years on the state sentence while doing my federal time. This meant I was eligible for parole almost as soon as I got to the state joint, and sure enough, after a short time at Four Mile I went before the state parole board.

I was optimistic going in to the hearing. I had made some positive changes in my life, and I figured once I told my story, the parole board would see that. I was finished with my former way of life and thought I should be granted parole.

I was wrong—way wrong. I told the parole board about the things I had learned and the plans I had for my life and my son's life. I explained that I was committed to living honorably.

But the parole board wasn't the least bit interested in my little story. They were far less warm and fuzzy than I had hoped, and they weren't at all impressed with my fancy talk. As far as they were concerned, I was a career criminal, a three-time loser who wasn't going to sell his bullshit to them.

Parole was denied.

Two things occurred to me as a result of the parole hearing. First, I remembered a quote from Emerson that said what we do speaks so loudly others can't hear what we say. I realized that the parole board had many years of ugly actions to balance against my pretty words. It occurred to me that my words were never going to convince anyone that I was changing the course of my life. Second, I realized that I was probably not going to be paroled anytime soon, if at all. I was going to have to serve the balance of my time, so I had better figure out what I was going to do for the next few years.

I was perfectly willing to serve a few more years, considering what could have happened on the state charges. I had been very fortunate, and I wasn't going to complain about doing a little more time. I had also come to believe that sometimes things that seem to be bad turn out to be good, so I was willing to let the situation unfold as it would.

In discussing the situation with my mother, I realized the best thing I could do was continue my education. If I was going to do a few more years, there was no point in wasting them. With the help of my mother and financial support from my grandmother, I was soon enrolled in school again. This ninth-grade-educated, high school dropout was now working on his MBA in management. *Sweet*, I thought to myself. *This Upside of Fear thing is awesome.*

But before I began working on my MBA, I needed some help. The education department at Four Mile was run by Captain Ed Gillentine. "Gil," as he was called, was not the typical career DOC cop. He was a damn nice guy who referred to his GED students as "Baby Boys," as in "What's up Baby Boy?" Gil seemed genuinely interested in helping guys find some opportunity. I think he probably had some hard times of his own when he was young, which helped him relate to the inmates.

I approached Gil and asked him if I could use one of the education department computers to do my course work. He explained that the computers were for students enrolled in the GED program, and technically no one else was permitted to use them. He then added that if I were very discreet and helped out with some tutoring, I could probably use one of the workstations in the back of the room. With Captain Gillentine's help, I spent a lot of time in the back of the room working on my degree. I had learned that help would come when I needed it as long as I stayed focused on my goals.

For the next two years I spent the majority of my time working on my MBA. Gillentine received the textbooks and course work and then sent them to me. I had access to a decent library, so I ordered outside reading and study material through an interlibrary loan program. The majority of my course work was reading case studies and analyzing various issues. I would then write reports outlining my proposed solutions and courses of action and send them back to the school for evaluation and grading. I took my education very seriously, and I worked hard to get the most out of the information.

After nearly two years of study, another vision manifested itself. I completed my course work and received an MBA in management—*summa cum laude*, no less. Amazing.

In addition to working on my education, I continued to work toward my goal of being a warm and loving father to Hunter by writing to him regularly. In 2002, I wrote:

My Dearest Hunter,

It's a beautiful, early morning, and I'm getting ready to go for a run in the sun!! It's amazing how sometimes the rising sun brings with it a feeling of renewal and hope. It kinda makes you realize that God is pretty cool!

Anyway, before I go for my run, I wanted to write you and tell you that I love you and miss you more than pen and paper can express. I have pictures of you on my wall that show you from about 1 year old to the present. Sometimes, looking at them makes my heart ache because I miss you so much . . .

Despite my heartache and regrets, I know there is a plan and a purpose to all this, and I know that one day you and I will be together as a father and son should be. What a wonderful time that will be!!!!!

Hunter, I love you more than any father has ever loved his son, and I am so very sorry for not being with you. Hang in there and know that I think of you <u>every day</u>. This will all be over soon.

Love, Dad

Although I spent most of my time studying, I was required to have a job as well. I got a job as "Law Librarian" at the Colorado State Penitentiary (CSP). CSP was the state's maximum-security facility and housed Colorado's new death row. I was bused in each day from Four Mile. The convicts at CSP were on twenty-four-hour lockdown and had no direct access to the law library.

To facilitate access to materials, CSP inmates had to send a "kite" to the law library. The kite was simply a written request for specific cases, statutes, or other resources. When I received these kites, I would retrieve the requested materials from the law library and organize them on carts for delivery to CSP inmates by the guards.

The process was hopelessly inefficient. When doing legal research it is sometimes necessary to read dozens upon dozens of cases in an effort to find one that supports a particular argument. CSP inmates were allowed access to only a few books at a time, so it took them months to sort through the relevant case law. Sometimes their frustration was expressed in editorial comments attached to the kites requesting legal materials. The comments regarding my limited intellect and family lineage were typically very entertaining and made for good reading.

It was a good job, and I enjoyed it. The hours were good, and it paid well for a prison job. I would go to the Four Mile gate at 6:00 AM and get a ride to CSP. I was usually finished by 11:00 AM and returned to Four Mile, where I had the remainder of the day free to study.

The only bad part of the job was going into CSP itself. The transport van drove into an entryway beneath the prison. I was then escorted through security portals, up several stories in an elevator, and into the law library located somewhere near the center of the building. Once inside CSP there were no windows. Chaos could break out in the world around you, and you would never know.

That's exactly what happened on September 11, 2001. On that day, events were set in motion that would forever change the world. That day also set into motion events that would signify the official end of my life of desperation, dishonesty, and impoverishment.

9/11 began for me like any other day. I was transferred to the bowels of the Colorado State Penitentiary, transported through the security portals, and escorted up the elevator to a windowless room completely cut off from the outside world. With no access to television or radio, there was no way to know of the attacks on America. As the planes crashed, killing thousands of innocent people, I continued my perfunctory duties of processing the requests of condemned men, oblivious to what was happening in the world outside.

About halfway through my daily routine, my supervisor entered the room and told me to wrap things up and that I would be going back to Four Mile early. There was no hint of anything unusual from him; we were simply finishing a little early.

As I left the law library and was escorted toward the elevators, I passed an administrative office where a woman was crying. I didn't think too much of it except that she was obviously upset. But I figured it wasn't the first time something upsetting was said or done to a female staff member in a men's maximum-security prison. These things happen.

After the short drive, I cleared the security gate at Four Mile, walked across the compound to the cell house, entered my cell, and looked at the television. My cellmate was explaining what was going on, but like millions of other Americans, I was having a difficult time believing what I was seeing on the screen.

As I watched the day unfold, the magnitude of what had happened settled on me. As I heard the stories of heroic firefighters, port authority cops, EMTs, and others who died that day, I clearly began to understand the selfishness and self-centeredness with which I had lived my life. I was struck by the fact that all these decent, courageous people were dying while I was sitting comfortably in my cell. It seemed strikingly unfair.

I had wasted the entirety of my adult life as a thief and a liar and a drunk, yet I was tucked safely away in my little cage, while others who had lived productive, useful lives perished. It made no sense to me. I had reached a point in my recovery where I wanted to be a father and a husband and a productive person, and it seemed wrong that the men and women who had done the right things were dying.

Over the next few weeks I came to understand what a menace I had truly been. I felt guilty about wasting my life and about causing harm to society. I was remorseful about my life before 9/11, but the events of that day magnified my regret for the things I had done and the person I had been.

The depth of my emotions surprised me. I was caught off guard by my reaction to a calamity that had befallen others. It was a signal that I was indeed seeing change in my life. I was developing empathy for others and not viewing events based solely on their impact on me. Perhaps there was hope for me after all.

A few months later I was transferred back to the minimum-security facility in Rifle, Colorado. There, I unexpectedly expressed a level of compassion I had never expressed before, and I got confirmation that my life had changed in extraordinary ways.

One morning as I talked on the telephone with my son's great-grandmother, Nana, a cop suddenly collapsed to the cellblock floor just in front of me. Instantly I hung up the phone and joined the crowd of inmates hovering over him as he convulsed and struggled to maintain his fragile connection to life.

Then he went perfectly still. As his life slipped away he began to turn grayish blue. I watched and thought how this was such a lonely way to die, surrounded by men who were totally indifferent to his suffering and by others who actually delighted in it. As he lay motionless, the cell house filled with screams and catcalls.

I stood there knowing I should do something. Anything. Even if I couldn't save him, was I willing to let him die right there without taking some action? Where were the other cops? Why wasn't someone coming to help? As I watched the jackals around him, it hit me that I was this cop's only hope. If that was the case, he was pretty much screwed.

Just like fifteen years earlier in the restaurant parking lot with Elliot, a fateful decision awaited me. What choice would I make? Would I do something, or would I just stand there? Whatever decision I made, there would be no going back—for better or for worse. If I chose to let this man die alone, I would forever cement my life of selfishness, misery, and despair. If I chose to help him, I might find a sliver of hope for redemption. What would it be?

In an instant I crossed the invisible line between good and evil, only this time I stepped in the right direction. After all those years of drugs, crime, and booze, I was given a second chance to regain a life of decency and honor. I seized the opportunity.

Under the critical and suspicious eyes of my peers, I knelt down next to Officer Mark McClure and began what could only remotely be described as CPR. I vaguely recalled taking a CPR class some twenty years earlier, but I couldn't even remember the number of breaths per chest compressions. All I could think was *Get some fucking oxygen to his brain.*

I thrust down on the officer's chest, recalling something about not pushing so hard as to break ribs. After three or four compressions I tilted his head back, drew a deep breath and breathed into his mouth. "Breathe, motherfucker—*breathe*!"

I tasted the Dr. Pepper in his mouth and tried not to gag.

I could feel the glares of those around me. I knew I wasn't endearing myself to anyone in the room, save maybe this unconscious cop who had forced me to take sides. *Goddamn cop*, I thought. *Just fucking breathe!*

Then a sickening thought occurred to me. *Any second now, a platoon of cops is going to charge in, and I'm the dumb ass over this cop on the floor. Jesus Christ, what have I gotten myself into?* Someone with a conscience had fled the building to get some help, but what would they do when they saw me leaning over this cop?

Just as I feared, I soon heard cops entering the building, yelling for everyone to clear the way. But instead of tackling me and jamming a stun gun up my ass, a cop knelt down beside me and said, "You do the breathing, and I'll do the chest compressions."

My nerves calmed a bit. I looked over and Lt. Joe Replogle was next to me. He knew real CPR and told me when to breathe for McClure. Finally somebody who knew what the hell they were doing was in charge. I just did what I was told.

After a couple of minutes that seemed like hours, Officer McClure gasped for air. He then began to vomit and slowly strengthened his tenuous grip on life. As other cops moved in to assist, I rocked back on my haunches and began to cry. I have no idea why, but I was flooded with emotion, and for some reason it brought me to tears.

I couldn't fathom the significance of what had just happened. Apparently, Officer McClure was not the only one back among the living. I was also part of humanity again. After fifteen years of living among the shadows of society, I was back in the light. This was the end of the beginning; it was now time to enter a new era in my life. What would the future hold?

Officer McClure returned to work after a brief stay in the hospital. Initially, there was no mention or acknowledgment between us of what had happened. It was, after all, very awkward for both of us.

I had been the recipient of much unwanted negative attention from the moment the event concluded. I was not living in an environment where saving a cop's life was considered a good thing. Indeed, the opposite was the case.

Fortunately, I wore on my chest what was considered an "old number"—the number issued to me following my night out with Elliot fifteen years earlier. The same number is issued upon each return to DOC, so DOC numbers serve as a benchmark in a perverse ranking system. The older the number, the older the con, and my extensive tenure in prison bought me some status among the other inmates.

Things would have been much different if I had been a "fish" with a freshly minted number. Men have died in prison for less than saving a cop's life. I had seen men beaten for simply conversing too often with cops, and my old number was the only thing that saved me from serious retaliation. After all, I was a three-time loser, and that proved my allegiance to the cause, right?

I don't think things were much better for Officer McClure. Having a convict save your life was like letting your wife protect you in a bar fight. Neither of us wanted a warm and fuzzy moment. The whole thing was better left unmentioned. But the conversation that eventually happened was a signal that I was, indeed, on the right path.

One night Officer McClure came to my cell door and very quietly expressed his gratitude for what I had done. He told me that he had a small child who would now have a Daddy as a result of my actions. He then told me that immediately following the event, an investigation had been conducted to find out what had happened and to ensure that I had not been responsible for putting him in his unconscious condition. The warden was concerned that I might have done something to hurt Officer McClure and then make myself out to be a hero by saving him—kind of a Munchausen syndrome by proxy thing on steroids.

Because I had been on the phone when he collapsed, there was a record of my actions and whereabouts during the time in question. As in any prison, the phone calls are recorded for security purposes. In fact, Officer McClure told me that when the phone conversation was reviewed, the sound of his head hitting the floor could actually be heard over my conversation. What he said next sent chills down my spine.

"Yeah," said Officer McClure, "at exactly 9:11 AM we could hear my head hit the floor, and you hung up the phone to come help me." I was stunned by his words. Could it be mere coincidence that the numbers that commemorate an American tragedy and my utter failure as a member of the human race were the same numbers that represented my moment of humanity?

I knew in that moment that I was on the right path and that I just needed to stay focused on positive changes. In time, things would get better, and I would enjoy the fruits of a productive and successful life. There was no way I could have predicted the awesome things that were just around the corner for me.

Following the McClure incident I received a letter from the warden recognizing my role in helping save McClure's life. As I read the letter, the warden's language struck me. It was almost as if the warden had known the words I had written on a piece of paper seven years earlier to describe the man I so desperately wanted to become.

In his letter the warden referred to me as a man of "good character." This was the exact phrase I had had in my mind when I visualized the man I wanted to become. It was not mere coincidence. It was more than that.

The letter went on to say, "You performed an act of heroism." It was stunning to read those descriptive words after the way I had lived my life for so many years. Somehow wanting so deeply to be that kind of man and focusing on it for so many years had resulted in it happening.

When I thought about the significance of 9/11 the date and 9:11 the time, and considered it in conjunction with the words used by the warden to describe what I had done, I realized I had become the man I had visualized. Furthermore, I knew in my heart that the rest of my dreams would become reality. My responsibility was to live my life consistently with those visions, and eventually they would come true. God would take care of the outcome if I took care of the process.

I thought back to a quote that said, "Destiny is not a matter of chance. It is a matter of choice," and I realized how true those words were. As I considered their implication for my future, I had to fight to control my excitement. I had a little more time to serve, and I could not afford any missteps. I needed to remain focused on my dreams.

I was scheduled to meet with the parole board a few months after the incident with Officer McClure. Over the previous two years I had met the board two or three times, and each time the result was the same—denied. I had come to accept that the parole board would never get beyond the things I had done, and no amount of talk was going to change that. I had read somewhere that "You can't talk yourself out of a situation you acted your way into." I understood and accepted that I wouldn't be paroled and that I was going to serve every day of my sentence. The good news was that with "good time" reductions, I had less than a year to go.

I had decided that I would not endure the humiliation of the parole board a final time and made preparations to waive the hearing. The parole board hearings were not about the future, they were about reliving the lurid details of the terrible things I had done in the past. I was tired of defining myself by those things, and since the parole board wasn't willing to change the subject, there was nothing to discuss. I had less than a year to serve whether I saw the parole board or not.

I discussed my decision with my case manager, Lt. Replogle. He encouraged me to reconsider my decision based on what had happened with Officer McClure and the warden's letter. I thought about it and began to wonder if my actions and the warden's letter might persuade the parole board to release me six or eight months early. Surely they would see I wasn't blowing smoke up their asses and that I was serious about changing the course of my life.

I also figured the parole board might actually want to let me out a little early so they could supervise my release into the community. If they waited until I formally discharged my sentence, I would be released with no supervision. Given my poor performance in the past, I figured they would want to keep a close eye on me.

I decided I would give it my best shot and prepared to meet the parole board one final time.

As the hearing date approached, my fellow convicts believed that I was going to go home. The conventional wisdom was this: save a cop, get a trip home. As I pondered the possibility of going home, I wrestled with the reality that I didn't have a home. I had filed for divorce from Hunter's mother, and although my divorce wasn't final yet, I was told my estranged wife had already remarried. Go figure. Apparently having two husbands was a minor detail for the blushing bride.

Where would I go if I were released? I had considered going to my mother's home in Louisiana, but that was too far away from my son. Hunter had been the primary motivation to change my life, and I wasn't willing to live 1,500 miles from him. Another possibility was to go temporarily to a shelter in Colorado Springs and try to get a job and a place to live very quickly. I felt this was my best option, so I decided it was what I would do.

The parole hearing finally came. As I entered the room, I knew I wasn't the same person I had been in the past. It was no longer an issue of whether I would change—in my heart I had changed. I was moving on with my life, and I thought the events surrounding Officer McClure combined with the warden's letter would clearly demonstrate this to the parole board members.

The hearing seemed to go pretty well, as we discussed issues other than my criminal past. The parole board could see the changes in me and would perhaps release me.

Then came the questions about the crimes I had committed fifteen years earlier. The next thing I knew I was answering very familiar questions about my night out with Elliot and whether I understood the seriousness of my crimes.

"Yes, I understand the serious nature of my past criminal actions. No, there is no justification for my behavior. I don't know if the victims of my crimes would want me paroled, but if I had to guess, I'd say probably not."

I wasn't the least bit surprised when Lt. Replogle called me to his office later that evening to tell me parole had been denied. That was standard operating procedure: case managers told convicts the parole board's decision after the board had left the building. I never understood why case managers were forced to take the heat for the board's decisions, and I'm sure many case managers wondered the same thing.

I was perfectly comfortable with the parole board's decision. Despite some frustration with the process, I could see things from their perspective. They hear the same spiel day in and day out, and there is no way they can tell fact from fiction. If I were in their shoes, I'd probably make the same decisions, although I would at least extend men the courtesy of communicating my decisions face to face.

On a Wednesday afternoon a week or two after my meeting with the parole board, Lt. Replogle called me to his office and told me I would be released to the halfway house in Colorado Springs on Friday of the following week. Just like that, it was over.

I struggled to make sure I was hearing him correctly. Did he mean that in nine days it was all over? How could this be? For two years, I had been denied halfway house placement every time my application had been submitted. I wasn't even aware that a new application had been submitted to the halfway house. It turns out that Replogle had submitted it as a matter of routine, and somehow they accepted me for placement.

This was excellent news. I would get out six months early, and I would have a place to stay while I found a job and a permanent residence. I couldn't believe it. I was going "home" even though I had no home to go to. That didn't matter; I was going to have my chance to build a new and better life, and I wasn't going to blow it.

During my final ten days of incarceration I thought back over the past fifteen years. I thought back over the bridge of time that began one spring night with Elliot and ended with saving Officer McClure. It was all so clear to me now.

James Allen wrote, "Circumstances do not make the man, they reveal him." That night with Elliot I had made a clear choice that revealed my true character. There was never any point in arguing that my night with Elliot was somehow uncharacteristic. The circumstances that defined my life in 1987 did not push me to commit a serious felony; they merely gave me the opportunity to show who I really was.

Likewise, fifteen years later, circumstances didn't shape my character; they simply revealed who I had become. On the day Officer McClure went down I had a choice, and my choice revealed, even to me, the man I longed to be. I had become the man I had dreamed of, and something deep down told me my life would never be the same.

In May 1987, I had stepped across a distinct line between good and evil. In April 2002, almost fifteen years to the day, I stepped back across that line to a life of decency, honor, and integrity. I had become a man of character, just as I had imagined.

The rest of my life now stood before me. I was thirty-eight years old, yet I was a child. I had squandered my youth, but I had been given a second chance to grow—a second chance that many receive but few capitalize on. I wouldn't waste my life this time around.

Over the past fifteen years I had watched myself become a man. I was the personification of a late bloomer, to be sure, but I had bloomed. I had committed terrible acts of dishonesty and violence as well as acts of decency and humanity. I had seen it all. I had done it all. Been there. Done that. Wrote the book.

I thought about the life before me and wondered what it would bring. I thought about my son and the responsibility I had to make his life better. I knew that the Department of Corrections would always have my name and number waiting for me. I also knew it would be there waiting for him. I had to give my son the opportunities and the life he deserved. I had to ensure he would never see the things I had seen.

I thought about the woman I would marry. Although I didn't know her, I had already seen her in my mind. I thought about what my life would bring, and I was filled with confidence and optimism. While the specifics of my future were uncertain, the quality of my future was cemented. I had seen enough of my visualizations come true to know that an awesome life awaited me, as long as I did my part and lived the life I had imagined.

As I left Rifle for the final time, I looked back over my shoulder at my former life. As the buildings faded away, I knew I would never be locked up again.

CHAPTER 17

Back on the Streets Again (Final Reprise)

October 2002 to April 2003

IN OCTOBER 2002, I ARRIVED at the Community Corrections facility in Colorado Springs for the third time in fifteen years. The transition facility where I would make a new start in life was a converted roadside motel that had always reminded me of the places my family stayed when my father's military career required us to move across country. All I needed was a Stuckey's Pecan Log Roll to make the trip down memory lane complete.

As a condition of my release, I was required to complete a forty-five-day residential treatment program before I could go out into the community and look for work. Although I had been clean and sober since 1996, the program was to serve as final preparation for my reentry into society. In addition to substance abuse classes, the program taught offenders basic life skills, from opening a checking account to learning how to eat healthy foods.

I was disappointed that I wouldn't see the streets for another six weeks; I was so close I could taste it. But I was grateful to be there. Deep down I knew I needed a slow reentry to ensure I didn't get sidetracked and lose focus on my new life.

Not long after arriving at Com-Cor, I had the opportunity to meet once again with Jarle Wood. He was no longer a case manager; he was now running the entire operation and several others like it. I had now known Jarle for many years.

As always, Jarle was firm yet soft-spoken. He was a man who had devoted his professional life to helping others turn their lives around. With his slender, scrappy frame and curly blond hair, he still looked more like a California surfer dude than a guy who spent his time helping convicts.

I asked Jarle why I had gotten accepted to the facility after three years of being denied placement. He didn't answer. He just smiled and said things have a way of working out without mentioning the telemarketing fiasco I had been involved in when I was there years earlier. Although Jarle never said it, I believed the Officer McClure situation had a lot to do with me being back at Com-Cor.

I thanked Jarle for all he had done for me, and I assured him I had made significant changes in my life. I would not squander the opportunity he and others had given me. As I left Jarle's office, I knew he was dubious—he'd heard it all a thousand times before. But I also knew that time would prove my commitment. I thought back to a conversation I had had with Jarle more than ten years earlier. He had told me I was the most self-destructive person he'd ever seen. I knew he was right, and I would have to be very careful not to sabotage my new beginning.

I spent the next six weeks doing various chores around the facility. Each morning I awoke early, often as early as 4:00 AM. I was so excited about almost being out, and I was so confident my life was on a new, uncharted path that I simply couldn't sleep. I had dreamed of this opportunity for so many years, and had come so close to never having it, that I had to make sure it was real. I wanted to savor every second of it.

Each morning I would get a cup of coffee in what was once the lobby of the old motel and relish the solitude of the quiet and darkness before others began the day. As I watched the headlights go by on the highway, I wondered where the people were going, and I wondered whether they knew how amazing life really was. I knew my time was coming. Soon I would be a member of the community of workers and taxpayers and responsible citizens. And although I had no idea of the resistance I might face, I was determined to create prosperity and a new destiny. I was thankful to be alive and (almost) free.

The closer I got to release, the more I realized how destructive life with my wife was and would be. She was stuck in the same dysfunctional patterns that I had lived in for so long. For years I had tried hard to make things work, since I believed a home with a mom and dad would be best for my son. But finally I hit the wall, and within a month or so of my arrival at Com-Cor, our divorce was final.

A few weeks into my new life at Com-Cor, I started thinking about a woman I had met in 1998. Her name was Janet, and she had been a volunteer in the federal joint. Fraternizing with outside volunteers is verboten in the prison system, so I never had any contact with her except during a few brief meetings. But even though I barely knew her, I often thought about her.

Janet seemed to be everything a guy could want in a woman, and I began to wonder what it would be like to have someone like her in my life. She was beautiful and funny, and she came across as responsible and trustworthy. I was so impressed with her that I had once asked her to befriend my wife. I believed Janet would have been a great influence on her.

When I first met Janet in 1998, I was still married to my son's mother, so there wasn't much sense in getting to know her better.

Besides, at that time I was a three-time convicted felon with several years left to serve—probably not the kind of guy who would interest her. But she intrigued me; she seemed to embody the kind of woman I had been visualizing, although I had always assumed that my son's mother would grow into that woman.

By 2002, that scenario had dramatically changed, and reality had sunk in. During the years preceding my release, my wife had become progressively more dishonest and unfaithful. I had been naïve to hope and believe that she was growing and changing right along with me.

As I thought about Janet, I figured I had nothing to gain by not trying, so I picked up a phone book, took a chance, and . . . bingo. There was Janet's phone number staring me in the face. *What now?* I wondered. Part of me had wanted to look her up, but another part of me was afraid I would find her.

After a lot of pacing and wondering about what I would say (and imagining her horror at being contacted by some guy she briefly met in prison), I picked up the phone.

Voice mail. *Thank God!*

While the message informed me no one was home and assured me my call would be returned as soon as possible, my brain frantically searched for something to say. Something cool. Something that wouldn't have her calling the police. Something a stalker wouldn't say.

Then I heard the beep and it was showtime.

"Hey, Janet, I don't know if you remember me, but this is Wally. We met when I was at FCI Florence. I'm the guy with the son named Hunter." Janet had a son named Hunter also, so I figured she would remember that about me. I continued, "So, I am out now and staying at a halfway house in Colorado Springs. There's not a number where you can call me, so I'll try you back later."

Whew! That was done. Whatever happened now, I couldn't be accused of not going after the things I wanted. I had wasted many, many years of my life, and I wasn't going to be stuck on the sidelines ever again.

For the next several days I resumed my daily routine of chores and therapy, but Janet was never far from my thoughts. Finally, I tried her number again.

"Hello," the voice said. It was Janet.

"Hey, Janet, this is Wally from Florence," I stumbled. From Florence! What the hell was I thinking? I wasn't from Florence. I was doing time in Florence. What an idiot!

"Hey! How are ya?" she asked in a Midwestern accent that hinted at her Kansas roots. She didn't sound frightened. This was good.

"I . . . I'm fine. I just got to Colorado Springs." I sounded like a total moron.

"That's great," she said. "Listen, I'm walking out the door right now. Here's my cell number. Call me back in a few minutes."

And then she was gone. I didn't know how to interpret our brief conversation. I had, after all, been in prison for seven years. I hadn't been doing much in the way of hitting on women, so I had no basis for evaluating how things were going. But she had given me another number to call. That had to be a good sign.

Unless it was a bogus number. I figured that a bogus number was pretty much standard fare to get rid of a stalker.

I dialed the number and a man answered. *Damn it, Janet!* I thought. *Just tell me not to call again. There's no need to play stupid games. If you don't want me to call, just be a grown-up and say so.*

Despite being played for a fool, I instinctively said, "Yeah, is Janet there?"

The man on the other end said, "Is this Wally?" This was really getting weird.

"Yes, this is Wally."

"Hey, Wally, this is Janet's son, Hunter," he said.

Oh! I thought to myself, *Janet's son, Hunter. That's nice.* All was not lost.

Hunter continued, "Yeah, my mom accidentally gave you my cell number when she left. Here is her number."

I thanked Hunter and hung up the phone. What kind of sicko game was this woman playing? I knew about strange women—I had just divorced one. But this was odd. Really odd. How in the world do you accidentally give someone your son's cell number instead of your own? *That ain't natural,* I thought.

What the hell. I called the new cell number Hunter had given me, not knowing what to expect.

A moment later Janet answered, laughing warmly as she apologized for her mistake. "I don't know what I was thinking. I was in a hurry to get out the door, and somehow I gave you my son's cell number." Her tone was friendly, and she didn't seem too strange after all.

We talked briefly and she told me she was on the way to an Air Force football game. I could tell she was short on time, so I took a deep breath and went for it. "Hey, maybe we could get together for a cup of coffee sometime," I said.

Instantly she responded, "How's your wife?"

"Actually I am pretty much divorced. Just waiting for the court to finalize everything."

"Then coffee sounds great," she said with a directness I wasn't used to. "Call me next week and we'll figure something out."

And that was it. I had done it. I wondered whether someone like Janet would be interested in an ex-con like me, but I soon learned that Janet wasn't into judging my criminal record. She was only interested in who I was today. My past was exactly that—my past.

Over the next few weeks Janet came by to see me several times. Each time she brought two mochas from Starbucks, and we sat and talked about life and the future. Janet had been single for quite a while, and it became clear that she was as interested in me as I was in her.

Things were moving quickly. Within a few weeks I sat Janet down to give her all the details of my life. I figured if the details were going to scare her, I might as well get it over with sooner rather than later. As we sipped our mochas, I told her the whole story of my criminal activity, beginning with my night out with Elliot. She listened and asked an occasional question. When I was finished, she gave a "whew" and said, "That's quite a story." I was enormously relieved. I had opened up and laid everything out for her.

My life was going well, and it could only get better. I thought back to that list on my cell wall and was amazed at what was happening. I had faced the fear of the robbery prosecution that had haunted me to the point of insanity for many years. I had earned a bachelor's degree in law and an MBA in management. I had sparked the interest of a beautiful, down-to-earth woman. Life was good. Wally was going to be just fine.

In January 2003, I earned passes to leave Com-Cor to look for a job. I stumbled into some part-time paralegal work, but I knew it was only temporary. I needed to find full-time, permanent employment, so I spent the next six months trying to find a job. This was easier said than done.

My criminal past turned out to be a terrible burden as I searched for work in a post-9/11 world. Although I knew what was in my heart, others had no way of knowing. Furthermore, instances of workplace violence seemed more frequent, and employers were sensitive about the liability of hiring an ex-con with convictions for violent crimes.

I thought back to the first sentence in Scott Peck's book *The Road Less Traveled*: "Life is difficult." I knew that there were no free lunches. I was determined to build a new life, and difficulty was no excuse for failure.

It was winter in Colorado, and I relied on the bus system and my feet for transportation. I trudged through the snowy, cold days from company to company determined to find work. On several occasions I got close, but as soon as I told prospective employers about my past, they politely showed me the door.

For example, I interviewed with a company that marketed insurance and securities. After I told my story, the interviewer seemed to recognize that I was sincere about changing my life. After a long talk he got up from his desk and left the room, telling me he was going to see whether an exception could be made about hiring someone with a criminal past. I saw a glimmer of hope.

He returned with some enthusiasm and asked a few more questions about the dates of my past convictions. His optimism was contagious. Maybe this was the break I'd been waiting for. He told me to sit tight then left the room again.

A short time later he returned with a grim look on his face. "Wally, I just can't get it done," he confessed. "I've tried, but it's not up to me." Then he asked a question that bothered me more than not getting the job. "What are you going to do?" It was the pity in his voice that got to me.

"Hey, I'll be fine," I said defensively. "Don't worry about me, I'm a survivor."

I left the interview late in the afternoon. The winter sun was already drifting behind Pikes Peak. It was cold as I walked the half mile back to a main thoroughfare to catch the bus. As I shivered at the bus stop, I reflected on the man's pity. *Did he know something I didn't know?* I thought. *Was my situation bleaker than I was willing to admit? Was I fooling myself with all this optimistic thinking?*

I watched the rush hour traffic back up and thought about the jobs and homes these people had. As the temperature dropped I envied their warm cars. I wondered whether I would ever really have these luxuries. I realized I was running late to get back to the halfway house. *Where is the damn bus?* I wondered anxiously. *That's all I need right now.* Getting back to Com-Cor after my sign-in time would have serious consequences. I couldn't afford to lose the only place I had to live.

Cold, jobless, and stressing out about the bus being late, I had my first real moment of doubt. Maybe I *was* fooling myself after all.

At last the headlights of the bus appeared in the distance, and I began to calm down. I got on and looked around at the handful of passengers. They looked as desperate as I was beginning to feel. I asked the driver why he was running behind, and he said he wasn't. On this particular route, the buses ran only once an hour.

I stared out the windshield, anxious for the bus to go faster. When we finally reached my stop, I jumped out of the bus and ran to Com-Cor. I burst into the lobby and signed in with only a few minutes to spare.

I walked to my room, sat down, and contemplated my situation. I had tried for several months to find permanent work with no success. I was frustrated and tired, and I was starting to question myself. Then I vaguely recalled something I had read years earlier. I couldn't remember the exact quote or who said it, but the gist was that our character is determined by how well we deal with adversity, not by how well we deal with success. I again thought about James Allen's counsel that "circumstances do not make the man, they reveal him." I reminded myself that failure was not an option, and if I didn't move forward I would be moving backward. Prison was backward, and I wasn't going there ever again.

CHAPTER 18
Epilogue
2003 to Present

IN APRIL 2003, I WAS FINALLY PERMITTED to go on non-residence status, which meant I could get an apartment and begin living on my own. I still didn't have a permanent job, but things between Janet and me were going great.

Janet had never left any doubt about how she felt about me, and I think I was pretty clear about how I felt about her. On Thanksgiving 2002, before I had earned a pass to leave Com-Cor for the holiday, Janet told me that she was going to drop by after enjoying Thanksgiving dinner with some friends. That afternoon, Janet arrived at Com-Cor, and I was summoned over the loudspeaker. When I walked into the lobby, I was overwhelmed by what I saw.

On a small table, Janet had deposited everything necessary for an authentic Thanksgiving dinner. She had brought real linens and silverware and an entire feast—right down to the cranberries. She even had candles on the table, although the Com-Cor staff wouldn't permit us to light them.

After my initial surprise I was a little embarrassed at the scene. Most of the residents had passes to go home, so there weren't many others there. Still, it felt awkward as other residents sat down in the room and watched us. Janet was oblivious to their stares and seemed to enjoy my embarrassment. She smiled and served Thanksgiving dinner as if we were in the comfortable privacy of a warm home.

Despite my uneasiness, I was as giddy as a schoolboy. Here was this amazing woman who could be anywhere and with anyone she pleased, yet she chose to come to a halfway house to have dinner with me. I had been getting to know Janet for just a few months, yet I hoped there would be a future together for us.

Over the next several months we spent a lot of time together, and it was clear we both intended to pursue this relationship as far as it would go. Maybe it was because neither of us were kids. Or maybe it was because we got along so well. For whatever reason, things sped up.

I thought about advice Napoleon Hill gives in *Think and Grow Rich:* if we stay focused on our goals, eventually they will manifest themselves in such abundance and with such ease that we will wonder how they had avoided us for so many years.

In April 2003, when I was allowed to move out of Com-Cor, it was no real surprise when Janet said I could move in with her. It seemed like the natural and expected thing to do.

When I moved myself and my meager belongings in with Janet, I was mesmerized by the warmth and privacy of her beautiful home. I had lived in boxes for the better part of fifteen years under constant scrutiny and supervision, and now I was in a home alone with this beautiful woman. It was a surreal experience after so many years of deprivation. There were no slamming doors or screaming convicts. There was no constant tension. There was no need to look over my shoulder. There was no need to dream of a better future. This was it. This was now.

At the end of the school year in May 2003, my son, Hunter, now ten years old, came to spend the summer with us. That fall we enrolled him in the fifth grade. He has been with us ever since.

I continued to look for work. In June 2003, I responded to a help wanted ad placed by a small heating and air conditioning company. I called the company and got an appointment with the owner for an interview.

As I had done so many times over the previous six months, I rehearsed what I would say. During the interview, I struggled to hide my desperation. Things went well as I worked my way through my sales and marketing philosophies, but then the discussion turned to recent employment history. I took a deep breath and laid out the entire story. I openly admitted my criminal record and quickly moved the discussion to the changes I had made in my life and my fierce determination to succeed.

As I completed my well-rehearsed monologue, I prepared myself for the usual response and dismissal. But the conversation took an unusual turn. After a few questions about my background and the changes I had made, I could sense this conversation was taking a different path. This interviewer wasn't excluding me because of my criminal past.

I left the company hopeful and optimistic. Certainly my burning desire to work hard and succeed was evident. No one in the world was more determined to sell heaters and air conditioners than I was, although I didn't know the first thing about them.

I waited for a day to hear from the employer, but no one called. Finally I called them. I talked to the owner and reminded him that I would do whatever it took to sell. He thanked me for the call and said I was one of three candidates being considered for two open positions. He was honest enough to tell me that because of my background I was currently in third place for the job, but he had not yet completed his evaluation. I would need to be patient and let the process develop.

Patience was never my strong suit.

Over the next two weeks I called every couple of days, trying hard not to be a pest while not giving him the chance to forget me. This was the closest I had come to a real job, and I didn't know how many more opportunities I would have to get work. If I didn't get the job, it wouldn't be because of lack of effort and persistence.

Finally, after two weeks of anticipation, I got a call. One of the first two candidates was not responding to calls so the position would be offered to me! I couldn't believe it! Finally, the break I'd been looking for. A job—a real job. A job where I could get up every morning and drive to work with a cup of coffee, just like the rest of the world. A job where I could facilitate a new and better life. Everything was panning out. I was grateful to Stephen Covey, Napoleon Hill, and Wayne Dyer for convincing me to write the components of this new life down on paper and glue it with toothpaste on my cell wall. Life was good and getting better every day.

I started my new job in June 2003, and approached my role as a salesman with great enthusiasm. During my years in prison I had read many books on sales and marketing, believing this would be my path to professional success. I worked hard, and in my first month I set a new company record for sales—almost $150,000. More importantly, I earned over $10,000 in commissions. Janet and I were excited beyond belief and began to see great opportunity for me in the heating and air conditioning business. And I secretly suspected Janet was relieved that she wasn't going to have a deadbeat on her hands.

Over the next six months I excelled at my new career. As I learned more about the business, I began to recognize ways to improve the marketing and sales strategy, and I presented my ideas to the owner. He seemed receptive and promoted me to sales manager, which allowed me to recruit and train new salespeople.

Over the first few months of 2004, as I led the new sales team to record-breaking production, I began to realize my potential as a sales trainer and motivator. I had spent years studying business and the sales process, and my personal story was a natural motivator to help others overcome their hardships and achieve unexpected success. Our sales team was comprised of a wonderful group of charismatic, dedicated men who worked their tails off for the company.

One man on the team, Winston Dennis, had a work ethic like I'd never seen in my life. He was a slightly graying man in his mid-fifties with a heart of gold. When I was promoted to sales manager and began reviewing applications, I recognized Winston's name in the stack; he was the call center supervisor who had tried to hire me months earlier. Winston was the first candidate I called about filling an open position. Although he had put in his application the previous summer, he agreed to talk with me. When Winston and I met, I realized that he was also the candidate who had turned down the heating and air conditioning sales job I was initially hired for. Now here I was trying to lure him away from his company, and both of us knew that I wouldn't even have my job if he had taken it the year before.

Winston came on board a short time later and became the foundation of our sales team. We developed a close personal and professional relationship that continues to this day. In fact, in 2007, Winston set a sales record of nearly $1,800,000 in residential replacement heating and air conditioning sales, and he remains our company's leading producer—as well as one hell of a guy. In 2008, he did it again, surpassing his 2007 performance.

It was at about this time that another of my visualizations manifested itself. Janet and I decided to buy a new house together, and we thought we should take about six months to find our dream home. Within forty-eight hours, we had put in an offer on a home in the mountains just west of Colorado Springs. It was a log cabin nestled in the pines of Woodland Park, the same kind of house in the same small town I had envisioned in my cell all those years before.

As my sales team solidified into a highly productive unit, I began to notice a change in the owner's attitude. Instead of celebrating his company's success, he seemed to resent me. In company meetings he insulted me in front of others, and he minimized the success the sales team and I were having. He seemed to have a deep need to take all the credit for our success.

I was beginning to realize that this man had an ego the size of Pikes Peak and wasn't able to share credit for success with others. I thought of a quote from Harry S. Truman: "It's amazing what you can accomplish if you do not care who gets the credit." Apparently, my new boss had never read this quote and preferred to undermine our success rather than give credit to others.

Within a few months the owner's bitterness and insults became intolerable, and I began looking for a new job.

It was then that another of my visualizations began to manifest itself.

Janet's family held a reunion every spring break. It gave Janet's mother, Jo Ann, the opportunity to get all her kids and grandchildren together. In 2004 the reunion was to be held, as it had been every year for many years, at a beautiful resort called Napili Kai *on the west end of Maui*, and Janet wanted me to go with her to meet her family during the ten-day reunion.

On the flight to the island paradise I thought back over my years of solitude and austerity and could hardly believe what was happening. Of all the places Janet's family could have vacationed, they had chosen Maui, the same island I had visualized and wrote about on my list of dreams. Amazing.

Janet and I decided to get married while we were there. So on March 18, 2004, we were married at sunset on the beach at Napili Kai. With Janet's family at our side, we exchanged our vows in a traditional Hawaiian ceremony, barefoot at the edge of the Pacific Ocean as the sun set in the west. A Hawaiian minister named Pia Aluli serenaded us with a beautiful Hawaiian song that neither of us understood. Wow.

Shortly thereafter I went to work at one of the largest and oldest heating and air conditioning companies in Colorado Springs. I was hired with explicit instructions to build a strong, well-trained sales team.

Over the next three months, I did exactly that. I pulled Winston over from the other company, and our new team formed a close bond. My team performed well despite the fact that one of the mildest summers in Colorado Springs's history drove down demand for air conditioners.

The owner of the company came across as a deeply spiritual man who professed his religion to anyone within shouting distance. In fact, when he hired me, he told me he was acting on orders from God. I was happy to have God as my advocate, but I should have known something was not quite right about this guy.

Disturbing signs began to appear over the next month or so. During funny moments in our sales meetings, the owner would call me out into the hall and ask me what we were all laughing about. He would then remind me that the sales team worked for him—not for me. I told him I was fine with that. I reassured him that I understood it was his name on the building, not mine. I realized he was a little paranoid and that he perceived me as a threat, rather than a guy who could help him reach his business objectives.

Ninety days later, the owner called for a meeting of the sales team—without me. I later learned that he asked the team whether they understood my sales system. They confirmed that they did. Later that day I was called into a meeting with the owner and his operations manager, and I was summarily dismissed.

The owner told me that he had been torn about what to do, but God had told him to fire me. Incredulous at his audacity to pass the buck to God, I said, "Are you serious? Didn't God tell you to *hire* me just ninety days ago? Do you really think he changed his mind that quickly?" Both men looked at me with blank stares. Although I was happy to move on, I was disgusted with their inability to take ownership of their decision.

I was confident now that I could make a living in sales training and sales management. I recognized an enormous opportunity in the heating and air conditioning business. The industry was highly fractured with large numbers of small companies and no sophisticated competition, and I felt strongly that a new company could compete and win a big chunk of market share. The only problem was that I didn't have the money to start a company and lacked the expertise required for the operations side of the business.

For the next several weeks I approached virtually all the major heating and air companies in town and tried to sell them on my sales system and my ability to lead a company to a number one market share position. Without exception I was quickly shown the door.

Exhausted and frustrated, I decided to open my own company.

So, in 2004, using credit card cash advances, we hired an operations manager and opened a small company in the living room of our home. Within three years we owned the largest residential heating and air conditioning company in southern Colorado. By the end of our fifth year, our little company had generated 20,000,000 in revenue. In 2009, the company was recognized by Inc. magazine as one of America's fastest growing small businesses. Amazing.

My life has continued to unfold almost perfectly according to the plan I constructed all those years ago in my prison cell after discovering The Upside of Fear.

I have recently started a sales training and personal development company called ITSUP2U Media, which is designed to teach others my no-excuses philosophy, help them grow their businesses and create the life of their dreams by embracing The Upside of Fear. I also deliver motivational and inspirational keynotes using the lessons of my life and the things I have learned to move others to reach their personal and professional dreams. In 2009, I shared the speaking platform with Dr. Stephen R. Covey who wrote the book that changed everything for me—*The 7 Habits of Highly Effective People*. I have done numerous events across the country with legenday sales trainer, Tom Hopkins. I am now in the business of writing and public speaking—just as in my dreams.

About a year ago I was invited to speak at Com-Cor and share my story with other ex-cons who were recently released. I have continued returning to speak at Com-Cor every month or so since then. During one of my recent programs I looked up to see Jarle Wood at the back of the room. He smiled and gave me an approving nod.

Incredibly, I have written this book on the lanai of my home in Maui.

Living an awesome life doesn't mean things will always go perfectly. We must learn to cherish life's successes and transcend the heartbreaks and struggles. There will be setbacks along the journey, yet we must persevere through difficult times. Even today I continue learning how to live life to the fullest in the face of adversity. In 2004, my sister Annette, who tried to help me in so many of my troubled times, died as the result of a self-inflicted gunshot wound.

Speaking Information

WELDON LONG IS AN EXPERT IN SALES AND PERSONAL DEVELOPMENT. Overcoming a 20-year cycle of prison, poverty and addiction, he has become a powerful speaker, a motivator, and one of the most successful entrepreneurs in Colorado. Within five years of stepping out of prison without a dime to his name, Long achieved emotional and financial prosperity for the first time in his life. All his dreams of success came true, including owning a multimillion-dollar business and beautiful homes in the mountains of Colorado and on Maui. Despite dropping out of high school in the ninth grade, Mr. Long now holds a BS in Law and an MBA in Management.

Weldon does more than write and talk about shattering obstacles and achieving success in life and business . . . he lives it every day. With humor and drama he moves a variety of audiences around the country to radically improve their personal and professional lives, and his edgy yet likeable style gives participants the motivation and practical tools necessary to break free from fear in life and business.

To learn more about how Weldon Long can inspire and motivate your team for peak performance, please contact:

ITSUP2U MEDIA
719.304.5300
info@weldonlong.com
www.WeldonLong.com